THE LIFE OF

PICO
DELLA MIRANDOLA

THE LIFE OF

PICO
DELLA MIRANDOLA

'A Very Spectacle To All'

BY ST. THOMAS MORE

This edition published in 2010 by
Scepter Publishers, Inc.
P.O. Box 211, New York, N.Y. 10018
www.scepterpublishers.org

Text design by Carol Sawyer/Rose Design

Printed in the United States of America

ISBN-13: 978-1-59417-109-3

CONTENTS

Introduction   vii

PART ONE: PICO'S LIFE AND LETTERS

1. The Life of Giovanni Pico   3

2. Three Epistles by Pico Della Mirandola, Two Written to His Nephew, Gianfrancesco, and the Third to Andrea Corneo, an Italian Nobleman   26

PART TWO: SPIRITUAL COMPENDIUM

3. Giovanni Pico's Commentary on the Psalm "Keep Me, Good Lord" (Psalm 16 [15])   45

4. Twelve Rules of Giovanni Pico Earl of Mirandola, Partly Encouraging and Partly Directing a Man in the Spiritual Struggle   54

5. The Twelve Weapons of Spiritual Battle, Which Every Man Should Have at Hand when the Pleasure of a Sinful Temptation Comes to Mind   61

6. The Twelve Properties or Conditions of a Lover   66

7. A Prayer of Pico Della Mirandola to God   74

░INTRODUCTION░

WHAT WERE THOMAS MORE'S RULES AND WEAPONS of spiritual battle? How did he achieve and maintain his famous serenity and good-humor? A close study of this puzzling *Life of Pico* will lead to revealing answers.

More formulated his rules and weapons of spiritual battle with exceptional care, in rhyme royal poetry, during what may have been the most emotionally trying period of his full and challenging life. More writes about this tumultuous period in one of his earliest known letters, a letter addressed to his learned and pious spiritual guide Fr. John Colet. More writes that he is brought "almost to the gates of hell" because of the many temptations he faces as a young man in London and because of the lack of clarity about his particular vocation. Yet, as his later life would show, precisely these early difficult challenges led to a personal training in virtue and to a lifelong commitment to prayer and ongoing spiritual practices that he sustained—and which sustained him—until death.

In another early letter, More complains that most then-popular "saints" lives were actually exaggerated fictions that often worked to undermine faith and to distract from the real challenges of good living. These faults are not present in More's prose account of the often-unsaintly Giovanni Pico, Earl of Mirandola.

Who Was Giovanni Pico? How Did More Know of Him?

Giovanni Pico della Mirandola (1463–94) was not only a rich, generous, handsome, and ever-cheerful celebrity of noble descent, he was also a genius said by some to rival the brightest minds of all time. As such, he was and remains, especially given his dramatic and short life, one of the most famous figures of the Italian Renaissance. Thomas More's greatest teachers— John Colet, William Grocyn, and Thomas Linacre—had all studied in Italy in the period of Pico's life, and More probably received Pico's published works from Colet.

According to his great-grandson and biographer, Cresacre More, young Thomas More took this "singular layman" Giovanni Pico "as a pattern of life" once young Thomas decided that his path in life was marriage. Yet this assertion raises many questions. Most importantly, why take as a model someone whose vocation was the religious life—which he neglected— and who as an unmarried layman scorned his duties?

This Puzzling Book

The puzzle of More's *Life of Pico* is evident from its very form: It claims to be the life of one of the most famous men of his times, of the Renaissance, but the biographical section is less than one-third of the actual book. And even this portion is an altered and highly abridged English translation of a much more laudatory Latin life written by Pico's nephew Gianfrancesco Pico della Mirandola. Throughout this edition, More's additions to Gianfrancesco's text are indicated by brackets: ⌐ ¬. Why did More make so many additions? And what did More leave out and why?

We will return to these questions shortly, after gathering clues offered by the second half of More's *Life of Pico*.

While the first half of this book contains the abridged and altered prose account of Pico's life and only three letters (also abridged and altered) of Pico's forty-seven published ones, the second half is mostly More's rhyme royal verse: "Twelve Rules of Spiritual Battle," "Twelve Weapons of Spiritual Battle," "Twelve Properties of a Lover," and a free rendition of "Pico's Prayer unto God." These poetic writings comprise what might be called More's spiritual compendium since they are an artful summary of principles and practices that More would maintain throughout the rest of his life. Most distinctive is the intimate and joyful love of God best seen in More's thirteen-part ballad on "The Twelve Properties of a Lover" but also in such seemingly insignificant details as More's adding the phrase "tender loving father" to Pico's "Prayer to God," a prayer that Pico addressed—before More's editing—to a powerful deity throwing thunderbolts.

"The Twelve Rules of Spiritual Battle" also focus attention on strong, joyful, and unwavering friendship with God, but only after More's typical common-sense approach in giving perspective. Rules 1 and 2 show that battle is necessary in this life for everyone, the vicious as well as the virtuous, and Rule 3 cautions that we not look for pleasure and delight when "Christ ⌐our Lord and sovereign¬ captain" led the way "by bravely bearing arms / And suffering bitter wounds" (p. 51). Rule 4, the longest of all the rules, focuses on Christ in each of its five stanzas. The first of these expresses the importance of joy and gladness, striving only for "⌐delight¬ / To be conformed and like in some behavior / . . . To our blessed Lord and Savior" (p. 51). The next stanzas stress the need in all spiritual combat to aim "with ⌐good devotion¬" to "resemble Christ," remembering how Christ "humbl[ed] Himself for you," even to the "most hateful and vile" death on a cross (p. 51).

Rule 8 reminds us that peace requires a constant battle but is ultimately a gift of grace. Such constancy presupposes a vigilant soul ever set on a victory that Rule 9 points out is never completely achieved in this life. Hence Rule 10 urges resistance to temptation from the first moment and Rule 11 gives the helpful advice that in particularly difficult battles one should consider that there is more pleasure in "hav[ing] conquered the devil / Than there is in any beastly pleasure" (p. 55). Why is this so? Because "The conscience draws more inner joy from virtue / Than does the body draw from any sin" (p. 55). This greater inner joy can be experienced even in the midst of the greatest bodily pain, Rule 12 explains, as long as we "consider how Christ ⌐the Lord, the sovereign power,¬ / For us did humble Himself unto the cross" (p. 56).

The necessity of remembering always the proportionate value of things is the major reason for More's twelve short "Weapons of Spiritual Battle." These "weapons" are maxims easily remembered and quickly recalled. The first is "Pleasure Little and Short" reminding us that "whatsoever delight" may attract our appetite will always be "little, simple, short and suddenly past." Or Weapon 3, "The Loss of Something Better" succinctly and memorably warns us not to be a "mad merchant" who "sells your soul" in order "to buy a trifle." But perhaps most powerful is Weapon 9, "The Peace of a Good Mind," which begins by asking: "Why dote so on these transient, worldly joys?" and concludes with the strongly rhymed[1] declaration:

You shall no pleasure comparable find
To th' inward gladness of a virtuous mind.

Then follow Weapons 10–12 recalling God's great love for us as seen in "The Great Benefits That Come from God," in "The ⌐Painful¬ Cross of Christ," and in "The Witness of Martyrs and Examples of Saints."

These spiritual weapons are used by the skillful and experienced to achieve "true happiness" marked by interior peace and joy—the biblical view expressed in "Pico's Commentary on Psalm 16." Although this commentary is entitled "Pico's," it is actually Pico's compilation of many others' traditional interpretations and is one of Pico's least characteristic works, a

---

[1] In the modernized text that follows, however, the verse is given as unrhymed iambic pentameter.

work compiled right after his conversion and never published in his lifetime. This traditional psalm commentary was also written shortly after a series of youthful dramatic reversals that Pico suffered and that led to his public conversion.

Psalm 16 expresses the traditional understanding of felicity or true happiness as the joy and peace achieved by loving above all else the living God (pp. 47–48). Here is the same idea, expressed in the concluding words of this commentary on Psalm 16: "Because all felicity of life consists in clearly beholding and enjoying God, we find next [in Psalm 16]: 'You will fill me full of gladness with Your cheer.' And since our felicity will be everlasting, therefore [the Psalmist] says, 'Delight and joy will be at Your right hand forever'—'at Your right hand' because our felicity is complete in the vision and enjoyment of the humanity of Christ, who in heaven sits at the right hand of His Father's majesty" (p. 49).

This "vision and enjoyment of the humanity of Christ" is the greatest happiness possible in life, but only for those willing to imitate Christ's life of sacrifice and service. But two prior habits of mind and heart are needed according to this "Commentary on Psalm 16": (1) genuine humility in recognizing virtue as a grace of God (p. 42); (2) genuine self-knowledge whereby we can recognize when in our desires we are substituting as an idol some particular good of life in the place of God (pp. 43–47). These are the first two points developed at the beginning of this commentary. When measured by such criteria, how does Pico fare in the prose biography as presented by More? As we will see, More invites us to be actively engaged in asking just such questions.

Troubled Youths of Thomas More and Giovanni Pico

After completing law school, More did not immerse himself in the many civic and professional projects which his well-connected father offered, but struggled to find his personal

and professional vocation in life. Considerable strife arose
between father and son—so much so that young Thomas left
home and not, it seems, voluntarily. During his mid-twenties,
More chose Fr. John Colet as well as the Carthusians as his
spiritual guides, learning the traditional ways of prayer and
ascetical life while working in London but also continuing
his studies especially in philosophy, theology, literature, and
history. During these years, More "made trial of himself" and
applied "his whole mind to the pursuit of piety, with vigils and
fasts and prayer and similar exercises." Finally, at twenty-eight,
he decided that his path in life was "to be a chaste husband
rather than a licentious priest."[2] He married that same year
and became fully immerse in family, profession, and society
while continuing throughout his life to spend the very early
morning hours in prayer and study. As time would prove,
More's father had rightly judged his son's special gifts and
aptitudes; their friendship grew and continued until John
More died at 79 in 1530.

Giovanni Pico never knew his father, who died shortly after
Pico's birth, and his mother died when Pico was fifteen, leaving
him a wealthy "master" of his own destiny (p. 12). As *The Life
of Pico* relates, his mother wished her son to be a priest so she
had sent him to Bologna at fourteen to study canon law (p. 5).
The biography does not relate that Pico's mother had started
her son on an ecclesiastical career already at age ten by having
a Cardinal obtain for him the title of apostolic protonotary.

---

[2] See Erasmus's "Letter to Von Hutten" in *A Thomas More Source Book* (Washington, DC: Catholic University Press of America, 2004). There Erasmus explains the father-son conflict in this way: "A liberal education [More] had imbibed from his very earliest years. As a young man he devoted himself to the study of Greek literature and philosophy, with so little support from his father, a man in other respects of good sense and high character, that his efforts were deprived of all outside help and he was treated almost as if disinherited because he was thought to be deserting his father's profession, for his father is a specialist in English law" (p. 8).

When free to do as he wished, Pico at sixteen began studying the "secret mysteries of the Hebrews, Chaldees and Arabians" and many other things few "had ever heard of" (pp. 6–7). These were—although Thomas More leaves out explicit mention of them—cabalistic studies, along with magic and numerology, which Pico pursued in his lifelong task to set forth the unity of all known quests for wisdom in a grand theory of "felicity" or true happiness. More also leaves out two well-known results of Pico's being his "own master": Pico was accused of heresy and briefly imprisoned; he was wounded and imprisoned for abducting the wife of Giuliano dei Medici. Nonetheless, young Pico scorned marriage as a restraint on his liberty (p. 18), and he officially remained under suspicion for heresy until the year before he died at age thirty-one. As master of his own destiny, Pico also scorned worldly business as mercenary and unfitting for a prince like himself. But what worldly business explains Pico's suspicious and unexpected death? More recounts only a sudden fever that not even the king's physicians could treat; he does not recount the rumors that Pico was poisoned by his own servants, those servants whom Pico's friends warned him not to corrupt by his negligence:

> His friends often cautioned him against utterly despising wealth, pointing out that this was discreditable in him and gave rise to criticism when it was reported, truly or falsely, ⌐that his negligence and indifference to money¬ gave his servants the opportunity for deception and thievery. (p. 17)

The Biography: "A Very Spectacle" of Virtue

In his original biography written in Latin, Pico's nephew Gianfrancesco presents his uncle as "a very spectacle" of virtue that all should imitate (p. 3). But was he? And what is More suggesting in this highly unusual work?

The original biography that More translates and radically edits was written by someone who is not always reliable and who based essential information on one of the most controversial and questionable sources of his time: Savonarola, that eloquent and gifted preacher who ended his life excommunicated by the church in 1497 and hung and burned by the leaders of his city in 1498. This source is never explicitly identified in More's version, although Gianfrancesco identified Savonarola by name and praised him as "this holy man, famous . . . for his learning as for his holiness of life" (p. 21). Of course Gianfrancesco was not intending to be provocative. The biography was first published in 1496, the year Savonarola was at the height of his spectacular power and reputation. But More published his *Life of Pico* in 1510, having worked on it in the early 1500s, shortly after his learned teachers and trusted friends—especially Frs. John Colet and William Grocyn—returned from their studies in Pico's Florence.

What More Left Out

From his translation, More eliminates one-third of Gianfrancesco's original text, mostly portions elaborating upon Pico's learning and his studies of the cabala and other obscure writings. (See note on page 9.) Besides eliminating Pico's excuses for abducting Margherita dei Medici, More also eliminates the opening letter and ending portion that encouraged readers to emulate Pico's virtues. Such modifications actually change the entire focus of the biography, from one of extreme praise of Pico as a master of his own learning and active agent of his own dramatic conversion to a focus on the question of virtue and a caution against overconfidence in having achieved it.

What More Added

This change of focus is evident in the book's very title. To the original, More added the lines within brackets:

> The Life of Giovanni Pico,
> Earl of Mirandola, a great lord
> of Italy, a man renowned for his learning
> in all fields of study ⌐ and for his virtuous life;
> together with various letters and other works
> of his containing much knowledge, virtue, and wisdom:
> whose life and works will repay being studied
> carefully and often brought to mind. ¬

Besides adding the topic of virtue, this title introduces the playful irony that will be present throughout the work. Notice, for example, the ambiguous phrasing of the bracketed lines: We are told that Pico is "renowned . . . for his virtuous life" and that the very few "letters and other works" that More edits for this collection contain "much knowledge, virtue, and wisdom" and that these highly abridged and edited accounts "will repay being studied carefully and often brought to mind." Of course writing that someone is "renowned . . . for virtue" is quite different from saying that someone *is* virtuous, just as saying that texts you have changed "contain" much virtue and wisdom rather than saying that the original writings *are* simply so. And why should these writings be "studied carefully and often brought to mind"? As examples to imitate or as examples to avoid?

An argument for the latter might be seen in the quite surprising ending, with Savonarola's report that Pico appeared from the fires of purgatory asking for prayers and, earlier, Savonarola's revelation that God mercifully cut short Pico's life because, having disobeyed—in the words that More adds—"God's special command" (p. 19), Pico nonetheless

did many charitable deeds and he did pray. Other such telling additions, to point out just two, are: More's adding the
phrase that Pico was "full of pride and desirous of glory
and man's praise" right after Gianfrancesco describes him as
"both a perfect philosopher and a perfect theologian" (p. 6);
More's adding the charge of "negligence" three times to this
biography (pp. 17, 23).

More's longest additions to the biography are the opening paragraph on the role of friends in helping each other to
live true virtue (pp. 1–2) and the long definition of nobility as
nothing else but real virtue (pp. 2–3). These paragraphs replace
Gianfrancesco's dedicatory letter which presented Pico as a
model to imitate, especially for his fruitful life and as someone
who "had won first place among all learned men of his own
day, not to mention those of antiquity."

The longest additions to the work as a whole are More's
highly original poems on the "Twelve Properties of a Lover."
Pico's version gave only a standard list of attributes of the
Petrarchan lover except that—following Pico's love for
Neoplatonism—the beloved is male. Then Pico gives six lines
stating why a loved one would serve his beloved, followed by
nine lines explaining that "these three reasons apply to God":
by serving God we are serving "nothing else than . . . our
highest good"; "he is the best and the most beautiful and the
wisest and has all the qualities that usually move us to love
someone and to serve him gratuitously"; and "he has conferred
the greatest benefits on us."[3]

The rationalistic tone of Pico's prose differs greatly from
More's ardent love ballad. Two stanzas are devoted to each of
the twelve qualities of a "perfect lover." The first part of each
expresses the ardent youthful love of a man for a woman; the
second applies that same ardent love to a dearly beloved God.

---

[3] See volume 1 of *The Complete Works of St. Thomas More*, p. 379 (New Haven,
CT: Yale University Press, 1997).

In the concluding two stanzas More gives his own emphatic "explanation" for serving one's beloved:

Serve God for love, then, not for hope of pay.
What happier service could you ever wish
Than that, which doing, is itself your good?
And who so kind, so lovely as is He
Who such great things e'er now for you has done—
First making you, and then upon the cross
Redeeming you with His own precious blood?

Emphasized in More's treatment is the lover's delight "In serving diligently, day and night . . . / For love alone." The "perfect lover will his love obey: / Ever is it joy and desire fulfilled / To put himself to pain what way he must" to show that love.

This emphasis on service and obedience stands in striking contrast to what we learned in Part 1 of *The Life of Pico*: Pico refused to obey "⌐God's special command¬" (p. 19); Pico boasted that philosophers like himself "⌐love liberty¬" and "cannot serve" (p. 34). This declaration of liberty of Part 1 with its extraordinary refusal to serve is directly contrary to the spiritual principles of Part 2, and it is one of the clearest indications of Pico's pride and lack of genuine self-knowledge.

Pride is never mentioned by Gianfrancesco as a danger that Pico faced; instead, he praised Pico for "perfect humility" (p. 16):

Oh how truly happy that mind which no adversity could darken and no prosperity make brighter! Not all the learning of philosophy could cause him to be proud; the knowledge of the Hebrew, Aramaic, and Arabic tongues along with Greek and Latin could not make him vainglorious; his great wealth and noble blood could not cause him to be puffed up; and neither the beauty of his body nor any great occasion of sin was able to draw him back onto the pleasure-seeking, easy path ⌐that leads to hell.¬ What could possibly be able to mislead the judgment of a man who now, as Seneca expresses it, had passed beyond the reach of fortune, disdaining her favor as much as her malice, in order to be bound in spirit to Christ and those who dwell in heaven? (p. 15)

Although the philosopher Seneca might believe that such detachment is possible, the biblical understanding—expressed repeatedly in Part 2 of this work—sees pride and attachment as a never-ending battle.

As stated in the very first point of the "Commentary on Psalm 16," pride is the "one peril" facing the virtuous person (p. 42). Pride is the great danger addressed in Rules 4, 7, and 12 of the Spiritual Battle. It is also the one theme that Thomas More would most develop in his subsequent writings.

Attachment to one's "chief good," one's own idol, is the second great peril (pp. 43–46), and since pride blinds, the proud have idols they do not recognize. The proud cannot have the self-knowledge to see how their desires enchant their reason and turn them to idolaters, worse than the beasts in Circe's power (pp. 24–26). Psalm 16 reminds us that many say "My God are You," but "there are ⌐very¬ few who can say these words truthfully" (pp. 43–44).

For attentive readers, More has designed his *Life of Pico* to help them "see" the workings of pride. How? First by leading them to ask and explore: What was Pico's chief good that led him to disobey God and to neglect his duties? In so exploring, attentive readers will ask, as More undoubtedly did: What idol(s) do I have? What prevents me from saying at all times, "My God are you"?

Attentive readers quickly discover Pico's greatest attachments: his books and his intellectual projects. One important bit of evidence is Pico's statement that nothing could make him lose his temper "unless it were at the sudden destruction of his laden bookshelves, crammed with the volumes he had taken so much trouble and care to accumulate." But he then goes on to explain that God would never allow such a thing to happen since Pico "labored only for the love of God and the profit of the Church" (p. 14). It is at this point Gianfrancesco gives that high praise to Pico's perfect humility.

Attentive readers also note that statements such as the following are simply not true: "Little store did [Pico] set now by any book except the Bible, and to its study he had determined to devote what remained of his life" (p. 16). As Gianfrancesco goes on to explain, Pico does not follow through on this resolution since "the common good prevented him because everyone was clamoring for the many and great works [Pico] had so long contemplated and labored upon" (p. 16). This rationalization must have struck More as quite comical, given the vastly difficult abstraction of Pico's work, work characterized earlier in this biography as so abstruse that few in the world had ever heard of it. As More's great-grandnephew John Donne put it, Thomas More had presented Pico as "a man of incontinent wit, and subject to the concupiscence of inaccessible knowledge."[4]

This rationalization also prepares us to discover why Pico did not follow "⌐God's special command¬" to accept his religious vocation. Why this failure to obey? According to Savonarola, Pico told himself that he must first "complete certain books" (p. 19).

What Is More Teaching about the Active-Contemplative Life?

Perhaps the most revealing answer to this question emerges from considering More's additions to Pico's "Letter to Corneo" (pp. 32–35). Corneo was a distinguished and close friend of Pico who urged the young earl to use his philosophy for public

---

[4] See John Donne's *Essays in Divinity* (Oxford: Oxford University Press, 1952), p. 8.

service. In his strongest declaration of liberty from mundane
duties,[5] Pico invokes the Roman poet Horace and appeals to
nobility and prosperity:[6]

> You write me that the time now has come for me to place
> myself in the households of some great princes of Italy, but
> I perceive that you have not yet grasped how philosophers
> see themselves. In their eyes, as Horace remarks, they are
> kings of kings; ⌐they love liberty¬; they cannot bear the
> proud manners of people of high rank; they cannot serve.
> They dwell within themselves and are content with the tran-
> quility of their own minds. Unto themselves they are suffi-
> cient, and more than sufficient. They seek nothing outside
> of themselves. Things held in honor among common people
> are not honorable in their eyes. Whatever men's lustful
> desires thirst after or ambitions seek, they set at naught and
> despise. And while all this applies to everyone, undoubt-
> edly it pertains especially to those so generously favored by
> fortune that they can live not only well and prosperously
> but also nobly. (p. 34)

Horace is a poet well known for his writings on duty, and
in the passage that Pico cites, Horace is actually satirizing the
very position that Pico has rationalized to himself: Horace is
ridiculing proud philosophers who consider themselves god-
like.[7] Although Pico misses the humor,[8] More surely did not.[9]

---

[5] In the biography Gianfrancesco did report that, "Natural inclination and the
study of philosophy both led [Pico] to love liberty above all else; and for its sake
he was constantly roaming and flitting about, never permanently settling down any
place" (p. 18).

[6] More seems to be redefining these two terms in this work. Consider the emphasis
placed on "godly prosperity" in the opening section he adds. Consider also the
long explanation of true nobility that immediately follows.

[7] Horace's *Epistle* 1.1.106–7.

[8] Pico does the same in his other use of Horace (*Epodes* 2.7–8) on page 18.

[9] The three Lucian dialogues that More translated and published in 1506 all satirize
supposed philosophers, ridiculous in their pride.

In his introduction to this letter, More gives what is ~~edly Pico's summary of Corneo's view of philosophy, bu~~ ᴍᴏʀᴇ adds a telling phrase revealing his own view of philosophy's place; Pico is criticizing Corneo's view

> that it is either servile or at least not princely to study philosophy for any reason except a mercenary one—meaning by mercenary all those things we do for pay or reward. Thus [Corneo] makes philosophy mercenary, treating it as merchandise for those who study it with an eye to what may bring him some material gain or worldly advantage, rather than as wisdom for the pleasure it gives ⌐or for instruction of his mind in moral virtue.¬ (p. 32)

What is the purpose of philosophy? The philosopher's own pleasure or instruction in moral virtue? More answers this question clearly and strongly in his "Letter to Gonell," written to his children's tutor: "philosophers . . . are the guides of human life," and the primary fruit of study is "testimony of God and a good conscience."

But how is one to balance liberty and duty? In this "Letter to Corneo," Pico presents his position, and by More's additions, we can most clearly see More's intentions in the work as a whole. Responding to Corneo's possible objections, Pico writes: "But just here you will say to me: '⌐It's fine with me that you study, but I would have you engaged with the world around you as well¬. I don't want you to embrace Martha to such an extent that you give up Mary entirely. ⌐Love them and do them both: study and worldly business.¬'" Here Martha and Mary refer to the active and contemplative ways of life seen in Luke 10:38–42. Throughout the rest of his life, Thomas More loved and lived both.

How Thomas More Engages His Reader

In his famous *Ars Poetica*, Horace describes the role of the greatest writers as creating "living words," words able not only to instruct but also to move and motivate. More's *Life of Pico* is designed to do just that. To any and all readers, *The Life of Pico* gives More's spiritual counsels and the dramatic story of a talented youth who begins a life marked by pride and lust but converts to a penitential and prayerful life. To attentive readers willing to exert the effort required, *The Life of Pico* can also lead to many other discoveries, including the deeply moving truth that any of us, by our own negligence, can let pride blind us to our deepest motives. In his design of this book, More our friend[10] gives us living words to motivate us to grow in virtue and in godly prosperity.

This Edition; Other Editions

Immense gratitude is due to Russell Shaw for the art and care he has put into modernizing this subtle and little-known work; his painstaking efforts will finally make this book accessible to contemporary readers—500 years after its first publication. The best scholarly editions for further study are Anthony Edwards' edition in volume one of *The Complete Works of St. Thomas More* (New Haven, CT: Yale University Press, 1997) and Jeffrey Lehman's 500th Anniversary Edition (2010) at *www.thomasmorestudies.org.*

Gerard Wegemer, Director
Center for Thomas More Studies
May 19, 2010

---

[10] Consider again the opening paragraph of this book.

THE LIFE OF

PICO
DELLA MIRANDOLA

'A Very Spectacle To All'

BY ST. THOMAS MORE

PART ONE

PICO'S LIFE AND LETTERS

❧CHAPTER ONE❧

THE LIFE OF GIOVANNI PICO,

Earl of Mirandola, a great lord of Italy, a man renowned
for his learning in all fields of study ⌐and for his virtuous life;
together with various letters and other works of his containing
much knowledge, virtue, and wisdom: whose life and works
will repay being studied carefully and often brought to mind.
Translated from the Latin into English by Master Thomas
More, who sends greetings in our Lord to his well-loved sister
in Christ, Joyce Leigh.[1] ¬

⌐IT IS A CUSTOM OF LONG STANDING, my beloved sister, for friends*
to exchange tokens of esteem or gifts at the opening of a New
Year as expressions of their love and friendship. This gesture
signifies as well each one's hope for the other that the year
ahead, having begun so happily, should continue no less well
and come to a prosperous ending.

Usually, though, the gifts friends exchange in this way
pertain only to feeding or clothing or otherwise gratifying the
body, so that one might suppose the friendship also to extend
to material concerns and no further. The love and affection of
Christian people ought, however, to be spiritual, not material.
After all, as the apostle says, "We are not in the flesh but in the
spirit if Christ abides in us."[2] And so, as a token of my wish

---

[1] A Poor Clare nun and member of a wealthy London family who was a friend
of More.
[2] Cf. Rom 8:9.

for your good fortune in this New Year, I have sent you, my dearly beloved sister, such a gift as may testify to my tender love and my eagerness for the happy continuation and gracious increase of virtue in your soul. Others' gifts tell of the worldly prosperity they desire for their friends. Mine tells of the godly prosperity I want for you.

These texts, more profitable than they are extensive, were composed in Latin by one Giovanni Pico, Earl of Mirandola,[3] a member of the Italian nobility. I need not dwell here on his learning and virtue, since hereafter I shall expound on the entirety of his life, though briefly, as suits my limited ability, rather than in a manner suited to his merits. The works are such, dear sister, that, for their size, I believe none can be found more profitable for instilling temperance in the midst of prosperity or winning patience in adversity, for despising the vanity of the world or desiring the felicity of heaven. I would have no hesitation in urging you to accept them—except that their good matter (whatever might be said of the translation) is capable of delighting and gladdening anyone with any scant desire for and love of God, whereas for one of your virtue, the fervent zeal for God is so marked that you can be counted on joyfully to welcome anything that speaks, even clumsily, in reproach of vice, in praise of virtue, or to the honor and glory of God. I pray He keep you safe. ¬

Giovanni Pico was descended on his father's side from the worthy lineage of the Emperor Constantine, by way of a nephew of the emperor named Picus. It seems likely that all Pico's ancestors bore this same name. But let us pass over these ancestors, ⌐truly excellent though they were,¬ on whom he conferred as much honor as he received. ⌐Instead

---

[3] The biographical sketch of Pico is the work of his nephew, Gianfrancesco, translated and edited by More, while the letters and verses are Pico's.

we speak of him—of his learning and his virtue. For these are qualities that a man may count as his own, and it is for them that he is more properly commended than for the noble blood of ancestors whose honor does not make him honorable. Consider: Either they were virtuous or they were not; and if not, then they were without honor, no matter how great their possessions were. For honor is virtue's reward, and who can claim the reward of virtue without the virtue to which the reward properly is joined? And if they were without honor, then how could they leave their heirs what they themselves did not possess?

Even supposing ancestors to be virtuous and, in consequence, honorable, they are unable to pass on their honor to us as heirs, any more than they can leave us the virtues that made them deserving of honor. Other people's nobility does not make us noble if we lack what made them noble. On the contrary, the more worthy our ancestors, the more vile and shameful are we in proportion to our falling-off from the worthiness of their lives. Their luminous virtue makes the dark stain of our vice stand out more starkly and conspicuously. But this Pico of whom we speak was so honored for possessing all such virtues that give rise to true honor that, like a body casting a shadow, he was a very spectacle to all who aspire to honor. In his condition they might behold, as in a clear, polished mirror, in what points real honor consists.

My poor learning is unable adequately to express his marvelous knowledge and excellent virtue. Still, if no one attempted to treat this subject unless capable of doing it justice, then no one would treat it at all; better, then, that it be done inadequately than left entirely undone. I shall therefore do my best to set before you briefly his entire life. And so, perhaps in time to come, at least I shall provide another man, better equipped than I, with an incentive for undertaking the task inasmuch as he is annoyed at finding the life of a man with so much learning recounted with so little. ¬

⌐His Parents and His Birth¬

This noble man was born in the year of our Lord 1463, when Pius II was Vicar of Christ's Church and Frederick III ruled the empire.[4] He was the last child of his parents—Julia, a woman of a noble line, and Giovanni Francesco, ⌐a lord of great honor and authority. ¬

⌐The Marvel that Appeared before His Birth¬

Before his birth an extraordinary sight appeared: A fiery ring hovered over the chamber where his mother was in labor, then abruptly vanished. Perhaps this was a sign that the child who in that hour was to come into the world of mortal men should possess wisdom with a perfection as perfect as that of that circle or ring; that his fame should be broadcast the length and breadth of the earth; that his mind would rise heavenward just as flames rise; that his fiery eloquence should in time come to worship God and praise Him mightily; and that, as the flaming circle suddenly vanished, so should this man's brilliance be withdrawn from mortal gaze.

Often we have read of unfamiliar and unusual signs preceding or following the births of distinguished, wise, and virtuous men, as if thereby marking out these special children in infancy, setting them apart by God's command from others of a common sort, and showing that they were born to achieve great things. Pass over other instances and consider the case of the great St. Ambrose. A swarm of bees flew about his mouth when he was in the cradle and some flew into it, then exited and flew heavenward, until, losing themselves among the clouds, they could no longer be seen by his father or anyone else. A writer named Paulinus[5] made much of this omen, interpreting it as a foreshadowing of the ⌐"sweet"¬ honey of Ambrose's

---

[4] The Holy Roman Empire.
[5] Paulinus of Milan.

⌐ "pleasing" ¬ writing that would display God's heavenly gifts and raise men's minds from earth to paradise.

⌐ His Appearance ¬

In face and body he was well proportioned and handsome, nicely built and tall, tender and soft, comely, and ruddy, with gray, dancing eyes, teeth that were white and even, and blonde hair styled in not too affected a manner.

⌐ His Scholarly and Humanistic Studies ¬

Under his mother's guidance and direction he was placed in the hands of teachers and began his studies. So eagerly did he apply himself to humanistic learning that in a short time he was accounted—and not without reason—one of the leading orators and poets of his day. He was exceptionally quick to learn and so intellectually gifted that he had only to hear verses read once to be able to repeat them, forward and backward, to the great astonishment of his listeners; and, what is more, afterward he would be sure to remember what he had heard. Usually of course it is just the opposite: those quick to comprehend are often slow to remember, while those who must put more effort into mastering things find it easier to remember what they have learned.

⌐ His Study of Canon Law ¬

At the age of fourteen, as directed by his mother (who was very eager that he become a priest), he went to Bologna to study Church law. After two years, however, seeing that the faculty cared for nothing except precedents and rules, he lost interest in it. Still, he had not been wasting his time, for in those two years, though still a child, he compiled a handbook or summary of all the decretals, wherein, as briefly as possible, he got to the heart of that whole huge volume and produced a work of no small value to learned and accomplished scholars.

⌐His Studies in Philosophy and Divinity¬

After this, as an eager inquirer into the secrets of nature, he left commonly trodden paths and devoted himself entirely to speculative science and philosophy, both human and divine. In pursuit of these matters (after the manner of Plato and Apollonius[6]), he carefully sought out all the famous teachers of his time, making it a point to visit all the universities and schools not only throughout Italy but also throughout France. And such indefatigable effort did he devote to those studies that, although still a beardless boy, he was reputed to be, and truly was, both a perfect philosopher and a perfect theologian.

⌐Of His Mind and the Vainglorious Disputations at Rome¬

He had been engaged in these studies for seven years when, ⌐full of pride and eager for glory and men's praise¬ (for the love of God did not yet burn within him), he went to Rome and there, anxious to make a show of his learning and little thinking how much envy he would arouse against himself, he put abroad nine hundred questions on diverse and sundry matters of logic and philosophy as well as theology. These were drawn with much study from authors Latin as well as Greek, from the secret mysteries of the Hebrews, the Chaldeans, and the Arabians, from many things derived from the old, obscure wisdom of Pythagoras, Trismegistus, and Orpheus,[7] and from many another strange source that up until then no one but

---

[6] Apollonius of Tyana, Greek Neopythagorean philosopher (ca. 15 AD?–ca. 100 AD?).

[7] Pythagoras was a Greek philosopher who lived c. 582–c. 507 BC. Hermes Trismegistus and Orpheus are mythical figures associated with esoteric and magical beliefs of ancient times.

a very few select men had even heard of, much less become familiar with.[8]

So that people would be sure to know what these 'questions' of his were, he posted them publicly, offering at the same time to pay the expenses of anyone who might travel from a distance to dispute with him. But thanks to the envy of his malicious enemies—envy, like fire, ever reaching upward toward what is highest—he never could manage to get a date set for his disputations. So he passed a whole year at Rome, with those who envied him never daring to engage him in disputation but seeking instead to undermine him, as if with hidden tunnels, through craftiness and deception; and that for no reason except malice and because they were, as many supposed, corrupt with pestilential envy.

The particular cause of the envy directed against him lay, it was thought, in this: Many who had devoted themselves to learning for years—some for the glory of it, some out of greed—feared that their fame might be diminished and the esteem for their learning reduced if so young a man, broadly educated and filled with knowledge, should, in the leading city of the world, begin to demonstrate his intelligence and his learning in matters of natural science as well as sacred science and on subjects others had not mastered in many years of trying.

Seeing now that they could not triumph openly over his learning, they brought into play the weapon of false accusation and put it about that thirteen of his nine hundred questions were suspect of heresy. Next they enlisted the support of some good, simple souls whose zeal for the faith and religious loyalties would move them to impugn the questions as novelties that sounded strange to their ears. Though some of the people were perhaps not without intelligence, in this matter they lacked sophistication and learning: for before then not a few famous

---

[8] Here More omits explicit mention of Pico's study of the cabala, magic, and numerology.

students of theology had declared their approval of these questions as being good and unexceptionable, and had testified to that by affixing their own names to them.

Meanwhile Pico, unprepared to accept the loss of his fame, composed a defense of those thirteen questions. This was a work of great erudition, eloquent and full of learning about many things deserving to be learned. He put it together in twenty nights; and there it is made clear not only that his conclusions were sound and consistent with the faith but also that those who barked at them deserved censure for their foolishness and ill manners.

To the most holy judgment of our mother the holy Church he submitted this defense and everything else he wrote. Having received it and duly examined the thirteen questions, our Holy Father the Pope[9] gave Pico his approval and showed him his tender good will, as is clear from a bull published by our Holy Father Pope Alexander VI.[10] Nevertheless Pico himself now desired that the book with all nine hundred questions and their conclusions not be read, since there were many things in it that were unusual and not fully developed, more suitable for private discussion by scholars than for public consumption by ordinary people whose lack of sophistication might cause them to suffer harm in this way. The reading of the book was accordingly forbidden.

⌐ Oh! Look upon the end of Pico's lofty-mindedness and proud ambition—that where he had thought to win everlasting praise, he had much work to do to keep himself upright lest his end be everlasting infamy and ill fame. ¬

---

[9] Innocent VIII.

[10] Pope Alexander VI did pardon Pico in 1493, six years after Pico submitted these *900 Theses*. But a number of these *900 Thesis* incurred Innocent VIII's threat of excommunication and order for Pico's arrest. Pico was not officially pardoned until the year before his death.

⌐ On His Change of Life ¬

As he told his nephew, however, he saw it as a consequence of almighty God's particular providence and singular goodness that he should have corrected his real errors in response to false accusations of wrongdoing lodged against him by people who wished him harm, and that, having wandered in the darkness, this experience should be for him a shining light enabling him to see and reflect on how far he had departed from the way of truth.

Before, he had craved glory, had burned with vain love, had been given to voluptuous relations with women. His attractive figure, his handsome face, together with his fame, his learning, his wealth, and his noble lineage, set many women aflame for him; and he, having decided against marrying and by no means reluctant to respond in kind, had fallen somewhat into loose living.

Awakened by his sudden setback, however, he gave up his riotous ways and turned his mind to Christ. Women's blandishments he exchanged for the desire of heavenly joys; and, despising the blast of vainglory he previously had sought, he set out now with all his heart to seek the glory and profit of Christ's Church. Henceforth he organized his affairs in such a way that even an enemy sitting in judgment on him would have had to approve.

⌐ His Reputation for Virtue and How it Drew People to Him ¬

Soon, therefore, the fame ⌐ of his noble learning and excellent virtue ¬ began to spread gloriously far and wide. Many worthy philosophers, indeed the most learned among them, hastened to him as to a marketplace of good ⌐ doctrine ¬. Some wished to raise questions and engage in disputation, others—of a more godly turn of mind—to listen and to absorb wholesome lessons and instruction in good living.

The lessons carried all the more weight because they came from a man more noble and wise than the one who previously had trodden the crooked pathways of delicious pleasure. Sound discipline seems most readily fixed in the minds of hearers when it is not only good in itself but is enjoined by a master who has himself been converted to the way of justice from the crooked, ragged path of pleasure-seeking.

⌐The Burning of Wanton Books¬

He burned five books of wanton love verses and other such nonsense, written entirely in the vernacular in his youth; ⌐for now he detested his former vice and feared lest these trifles might later be the occasion of some evil. ¬

⌐His Study and Diligence in Sacred Scripture¬

From this time on he devoted himself day and night to the fervent study of Scripture,[11] ⌐writing a number of noble books that testify to his angelic quickness, his ardent labor, and his profound erudition; some of these we have and some—a treasure beyond estimation—we have lost. It is amazing to think how rapidly he read through huge collections of books and copied out what suited him.

His knowledge of the ancient Fathers of the Church was so extensive that only with difficulty could a man have acquired it who had done nothing else in a long lifetime except read them. As for the more recent theologians, he knew them so well that one might think he knew everything there was to know in them and had it all as fresh in mind as if even then poring over their works. Among these more recent scholars, he especially commended Saint Thomas as one who stood out as a sure pillar of truth in his own right. ¬

---

[11] Here More omits roughly one-third of the original text, summarizing in the section that follows Pico's special studies and writings.

He was very quick-witted, wise, and subtle in disputations and, in the days when he was still of a fiery temperament, found them a great source of felicity. By now, though, he had long since bade farewell to these contests. Every day he hated them more, and so greatly did he abhor them that when Ercole d'Este, Duke of Ferrara, asked him—first by messengers and then in his own person—to come to Ferrara and engage in a disputation on the occasion of a general chapter of the Friars Preacher,[12] it took a great deal of persuading to get him there. But the Duke, who was most especially fond of him, insisted, and finally he came, conducting himself so splendidly that it was wonderful to see how much the entire audience enjoyed hearing him, for no man could have spoken more learning more learnedly.

Still, he was accustomed to say such skirmishes were suitable for a logician, not a philosopher. He said, too, that the disputations that were highly profitable were those conducted peacefully and in private, in a search for truth carried on without a large audience present.

As for public disputations staged openly to show off learning and win the favor of common people and the praise of fools, he said they did much harm. Together with the desire of themselves being admired, for which these silly disputants are so eager, he considered inseparably joined the intention of causing embarrassment and rebuke to him with whom they dispute; and this intention is the soul's moral wounding and deadly poison. None of those contentious quibbles and hair-splitting sophistries escaped his attention, nor was there anything he more hated and despised, holding that they served no purpose except to shame men more truly learned in serious studies and ignorant of those trifles, while contributing little or nothing to the quest for truth that was his constant occupation.

---

[12] The Dominicans.

⌐ His Universal Learning ¬

Wishing not to delay the reader any longer, however, we shall say but a word or two of a general nature about his learning.

Some men have distinguished themselves in eloquence yet been shamed by their ignorance of natural philosophy. Some have shone by their familiarity with various strange tongues but lacked any knowledge of philosophy. Some have read the entire output of the philosophers of old but known nothing of new thinking. And some have sought learning in both philosophy and theology for the sake of praise and vainglory rather than the profit and building up of Christ's Church. Pico, however, devoted himself to all these disciplines as if filled to the brim by a great torrent of learning.

Unlike the state of those people who set everything else aside in order to be excellent in one thing, he progressed so much in all fields of study that, no matter by which you measured him, you would have supposed it his sole object of study. And still more remarkable in him was it that, ⌐ for the love of God and the profit of His Church, ¬ he achieved all this by the power of his own intellect, without teachers. Thus we can say of him what the philosopher Epicurus said of himself: He was his own master.

⌐ Five Causes of His Achieving Such Remarkable Learning in So Short a Time ¬

Five causes appear to me to converge to produce such remarkable results in so little time: first, a powerful intelligence; second, a notably retentive memory; third, great wealth, which was extremely helpful to him for buying books in Latin, Greek, and other languages (he spent seven thousand ducats on a collection of volumes of all kinds); fourth, his steady, indefatigable application to study; and fifth, his contempt or indifference toward everything earthbound.

⌐ Of His Conditions and His Virtue ¬

Now, though, let us leave those powers of his soul that have to do with understanding and knowledge, and speak of those that pertain to the doing of noble deeds; let us affirm his excellent conditions as well as we can, so that his mind's ardor for God may be seen and the giving of his riches to the poor may be understood. The purpose is that those ⌐who hear of his virtue¬ may thereby be moved to praise it in particular and give thanks for it to almighty God, from whose infinite goodness come all grace and virtue.

⌐ The Sale of His Properties. His Alms ¬

Three years before his death he sold all his patrimony and lands—that is, a third of the earldom of Mirandola and Concordia—to his nephew Gianfrancesco,[13] and for so little that it seemed more gift than sale. It was his aim that, having put aside all the burden and business of rule or lordship, and being fully aware of the end to which earthly honors and worldly dignities come at the last, he might live in tranquility and peace.

Part of whatever he got from his transaction he gave away to the poor, and part he used to buy a little land to support himself and his household. He also distributed among poor people a great quantity of silver vessels and plates along with other precious and costly household utensils. At table he was content with simple fare, while still retaining something of the old custom of serving many dainty dishes and using silver vessels. Daily at set times he devoted himself to prayer.

To poor men, if they came by, he always gave ⌐generously¬ of his money; and, not satisfied with merely giving what he already had, he wrote to one Girolamo Benivieni—a Florentine

---

[13] Gianfrancesco Pico is, of course, the author of this biography, and the one to whom Pico writes the letters that follow in More's edition.

and a well-educated man of whom he was particularly fond for the notable affection shown him by Benivieni as well as for his upright character—telling him that if he should happen to spend anything to help the poor and provide maidens with dowries, he should let Pico know about it and Pico would reimburse him. This was so that by way of Benievieni as by a faithful agent he might relieve the needs and lighten the burdens of needy people of whom he himself was unaware.

⌐The Voluntary Afflicting and Punishment of His Own Body¬

Over and above all this he often—and it should not be kept a secret—'gave alms' in his own body. We know many men who, as Saint Jerome says, extend help to the poor while at the same time they are overcome by the pleasures of the flesh. But many days—and specifically those days that recall Christ's passion and death for our sakes—Pico beat and scourged his flesh in remembrance of that great act of generosity and in reparation for his former offenses.

⌐His Amiability and Good Nature¬

He was consistently cheerful, so equable of temperament that anger never troubled him. He once told his nephew that whatever might happen—no matter how great a misfortune—he believed himself incapable of becoming wrathful, unless it were at the sudden destruction of his laden bookshelves, crammed with the volumes he had taken so much trouble and care to accumulate.

Certain as he was, however, that he labored only for the love of God and the profit of His Church, and to Him dedicated all his work, his studies, and his activities, and knowing that ⌐due to God's omnipotence¬ his efforts could not come to naught unless God commanded it or allowed it, his sense of ⌐God's all-goodness¬ gave him confidence that the Almighty would not visit such suffering upon him.

Oh how truly happy that mind which no adversity could darken and no prosperity make brighter! Not all the learning of philosophy could cause him to be proud; the knowledge of the Hebrew, Aramaic, and Arabic tongues along with Greek and Latin could not make him vainglorious; his great wealth and noble blood could not cause him to be puffed up; and neither the beauty of his body nor any great occasion of sin was able to draw him back onto the pleasure-seeking, easy path ⌐that leads to hell.¬ What could possibly be able to mislead the judgment of a man who now, as Seneca expresses it, had passed beyond the reach of fortune, disdaining her favor as much as her malice, in order to be bound in spirit to Christ and those who dwell in heaven?

⌐How He Refused Positions of Honor¬

Seeing that many men go to great trouble and expense to seek, and are avid to purchase, ecclesiastical offices and dignities—which nowadays, alas, are commonly bought and sold—he declined these when offered by two kings. When another man offered him great worldly advancement if he would go to the King's court, he answered in such a way as to leave no doubt that he desired neither admiring notice nor worldly riches, but instead set them at naught so that he might more undisturbedly devote himself to study and to God's service. For he was certain that it was praiseworthy in a philosopher and a seeker of wisdom not to acquire riches but to refuse them.

⌐The Despising of Worldly Glory¬

All human praise and earthy glory he deemed worthless. Yet in rejecting this shadow-glory, he strove for true glory, which ever attends upon virtue as its inseparable servant. Fame, he said, often harmed men while they were alive and never did them any good after they were dead. He attached importance to his

learning to the extent it was profitable to the Church and for
the extermination of errors. Beyond that, he had reached such
a degree of perfect humility that he hardly cared whether or
not his works were published under his own name as long as
they accomplished as much good as if they were.

Little store did he set now by any book except the Bible,
and to its exclusive study he had determined to devote what
remained of his life; except that the common good prevented
him inasmuch as everyone was clamoring for those many great
works he had so long contemplated and labored upon.

⌐How Much More Highly He Valued Devotion than Learning¬

More than his own knowledge of things of nature and things of
God, he valued the modest inclination of an old man or woman
toward God, however slight it might be. When communicating
with his close friends, he often would remind them how everything mortal declines and comes to an end, how uncertain and
transitory are the things of this present life, how settled and
stable our future life will be, whether we be cast down into
hell or raised up to heaven. And on these grounds he exhorted
them to raise their minds to the love of God, something far
more excellent than all the learning we can possibly acquire in
this life.

This same subject he touches on in the book he called *De
Ente et Uno*. There, interrupting his argument and addressing
Angelo Poliziano,[14] to whom the book is dedicated, he writes:
"But see now, my well-loved Angel, what madness grips us.
Better it is, as long as we are in the body, that we love God
than either know Him or speak of Him. In loving Him we also
profit ourselves more, labor less, and do Him more service; and
failing to find what we seek by intellectual knowledge is always

---

[14] Angelo Poliziano (1454–1494): close friend of Pico, poet and humanist.

better than the possessing by love that which it would be use-less to find except that we loved it."

⌐His Liberality and Contempt for Riches¬

The only thing excessive about him was his liberality: for so far removed was he from taking any heed of earthly things that he seemed somewhat marred by the blemish of ⌐negligence¬.[15] His friends often cautioned him against utterly despising wealth, pointing out that this was discreditable in him and gave rise to criticism when it was reported, truly or falsely, ⌐that his negligence and indifference to money¬ gave his servants the opportunity for deception and thievery. Yet his mind, con-stantly raised to the contemplation of heavenly things and the searching out of nature's wisdom, even so could never lower itself to the consideration and oversight of these base, abject, vile earthly things.

One day his chief steward came to him and, asking that he hear an accounting for money received from him over a period of some years, brought out his ledgers. Pico replied in this vein: "My friend, I am well aware that you could have deceived me many times in the past and can do so in the future if you care to. It serves no good purpose to examine these expenses. ⌐There is no more to do:¬ if I owe you something, I shall pay you by and by; and if you owe me, pay me—now if you can do it or later if you can't manage it now."

⌐His Loving Mind and Virtuous Behavior toward His Friends¬

With great kindness ⌐and courtesy¬ he entreated his friends and ⌐loved ones,¬ and was accustomed privately to exhort them to turn to God. His godly words had ⌐such a great impact

---

[15] This is the first of three times More adds "negligence" as Pico's dominant fault; see later in this paragraph and also the second last paragraph of this *Life*.

on those to whom they were addressed ¬ that one day, when a ⌐learned¬ man ⌐(less good than learned) came ¬ to consult him, drawn by his reputation for scholarship, Pico had spoken scarcely two words to him on the subject of virtue before, pierced to the heart, he immediately abandoned the practice of vice and reformed his character. This is what Pico said to him: "If we kept steadily before our eyes the ⌐painful¬ death that Christ suffered for love of us, and then turned our thoughts to our own death, we would surely have a horror of sin."

His notable kindness and courtesy were not shown to those who had great strength of body or wealth, but to those whose learning and good condition drew him to them. For similarity in the way people live is a cause of love and friendship; as Apollonius remarks, likeness of condition is itself affinity.

⌐What He Hated and What He Loved¬

Nothing was more odious and intolerable to him than what Horace speaks of as the proud palaces of stately lords. He was nearly as disinclined to marry as to engage in worldly affairs. On one occasion, nevertheless, laughingly asked which of these two burdens he considered lighter and would sooner choose if a choice had to be made, he thought for a moment, then finally shook his head and, smiling slightly, replied that he would sooner marry, since there were in it less servitude and less danger.

Natural inclination and the study of philosophy both led him to love liberty above all else; and for its sake he was constantly roaming and flitting about, never permanently settling down any place.

⌐His Fervent Love of God¬

 He did not attach much importance to outward observances. Here we do not speak of those observances which the Church commands, for in those he was diligent, but of those ceremonies people invent, while setting aside the true service of God, Who, ⌐as Christ says,¬ should be worshiped in spirit and deed. But in the inner affections of his heart he clung to God with very fervent love and ⌐devotion¬.

At times that great enthusiasm flagged and nearly vanished, but then it would once more surge up powerfully toward God. So ardently did the love of God burn in him that on one occasion, walking in an orchard at Ferrara with his nephew Gianfrancesco and speaking of the love of Christ, he burst out thus: "Nephew, let me tell you something that I charge you to keep to yourself. Once I have completed certain books, I intend to give the poor whatever substance I have left and, with the crucifix as my protection, go barefoot about the world, preaching Christ in every town and castle." I understand that later, ⌐acting at God's special command,¬ he changed that resolution and determined to be professed in the order of Friars Preacher.

⌐His Death¬

In the year of our redemption 1494, having completed his thirty-first year and then living at Florence, he was suddenly seized by a burning fever that so pervaded his inner organs as to resist all medicines and withstand all cures, and obliged him in just three days to succumb to nature and ⌐render back to her the life he had received from her.¬

⌐His Behavior as His Life Drew to a Close¬

After he had received the holy Body of our Savior, they placed the crucifix before him, so that before surrendering his spirit, he might drink deeply of love and compassion while gazing upon that pitiful figure as a powerful defense against all adversity and a sure rampart against wicked spirits. The priest asked him whether he firmly believed that the crucifix was an image of Him who was true God and true man; that in his Godhead

He was begotten before all time of His Father, to Whom He is also equal in all things; and that by the Holy Spirit, also God, Who proceeds from Him and from the Father—the three Persons being one God—He was conceived in time in the chaste womb of our Lady, a perpetual Virgin; that He suffered hunger, thirst, heat, ⌐cold,¬ labor, struggle, and care; and that finally, to wash away the stain of sin which we contracted and made our own through Adam's sin, he willingly, gladly shed His most precious blood on the altar of the cross out of His sovereign love for mankind.

The priest, I say, asked him these and other such things as they are wont to put to people in this situation; and Pico answered that he not only believed them but also knew them with certainty. His sister's son Alberto, a young man of intelligence, learning, and excellent conditions, began to console him as one facing death and, using arguments of natural reason, to show him why death was not to be feared but embraced as that which finally puts an end to all the labor, pain, trouble, and sorrow of this short, miserable, ⌐death-bound¬ life. Pico replied that it was not just for the realization that death terminates life's many miseries and painful wretchedness that, mainly, he was content to die; rather, his contentment lay in the realization that death's approach calls a halt to sinning: for the brief span of life left to him afforded no time for committing sin and offending. He also asked forgiveness of all his servants if he had offended any of them in time past. ⌐Eight¬ years before he had provided for them in his will: food and drink for some, money for some, for each what he deserved.

To this same Alberto and many other reliable persons he also disclosed that the Queen of heaven had come to him that night, exuding a remarkably fragrant odor that refreshed his frame and limbs, bruised and crushed as they were by fever, and had promised him that his death would not be the absolute, final end. His countenance as he lay there was continually pleasant and cheerful, and amid the very toils and pangs of death he spoke as if he beheld the heavens opening. All who came and greeted him, offering their service, he received with very loving words, thanked, and kissed.

He designated his brother Antonio as executor of his moveable property. The poor people of the almshouse of Florence he named heirs of his lands. ⌐And in this manner did he give up his spirit into the hands of our Savior.¬

⌐How His Death Was Received¬

With what sadness and heaviness of heart his passing out of this world was received by rich and poor, high and low, the princes of Italy well testify, the cities and people well give witness, the great kindness and singular courtesy of King Charles of France well shows forth.[16]

For approaching Florence and intending to go to Rome from there and then on to his expedition against Naples, the King, hearing of Pico's illness, sent two of his own physicians to him in his name to help him as much as they could. Besides that, Charles sent him letters, signed by his own hand, and filled with such humane and courteous offers as the benevolent mind of so worthy a prince and Pico's eminent virtues required.

⌐The State of His Soul¬

⌐Not long after Pico's death,¬ Friar Girolamo,[17] a Dominican of Ferrara and a man as famous for his learning as for his holiness of life, spoke as follows to the people in a sermon preached in Florence's principal church:[18]

> "City of Florence, I have a secret to share with you that is as true as the gospel of St. John. I would have kept it a secret,

---

[16] King Charles VIII (1470–1498).

[17] Girolamo Savonarola (1452–1498).

[18] The Duomo.

but I am obliged to divulge it because he who has authority to command me has so instructed me.

"None of you, I suppose, is unacquainted with Giovanni Pico, Earl of Mirandola, a man in whom God heaped up many great gifts and singular graces. The Church suffered an inestimable loss by his death, for had he been granted longer life, he would have excelled by the works he left behind him all who have lived and died during these last eight hundred years.

"It was Pico's custom to speak with me and share the secrets of his heart, and in this manner I came to see that God by private inspiration was calling him to the religious state. And Pico for his part often resolved to heed this inspiration and respond to his calling. Yet, insufficiently grateful for God's great blessings or held back by the weakness of the flesh—and he was a person of tender constitution—he shrank from the effort. Or thinking perhaps that religious life had no need for him, he put off taking that step for a time. But I admit that in saying these things I am guessing.

"Throughout two whole years, in any case, I warned him that he would be punished if he failed to act on that intention God had put in his mind. Certainly, too—I don't deny it—I prayed God to send him some chastisement that would compel him to set upon the path God had opened to him. But I did not desire him to be scourged with the scourge that has been visited on him. I did not look for that. Yet our Lord has decreed that he should leave this present life and lose a portion of that noble crown that he should have received in heaven.

"Even so, the most benign Judge has dealt most mercifully with him. For the plentiful alms he dispensed to the poor with a free and liberal hand and the devout prayers he constantly offered to God, he has been granted this favor: Although his soul does not yet know heavenly joy in the bosom of our Lord, neither is it condemned to perpetual pain; he is consigned for a while to the fire of purgatory and there will suffer pain for a certain time only. And I am still more glad to tell you this in order that those who knew him well, especially those so singularly in his debt for his many generous deeds, should now help him by their prayers, alms-giving, and other acts of intercession."

These things were publicly affirmed by this holy man Girolamo, who also declared himself well aware that if he were to lie in that holy place he would deserve eternal damnation. And, what is more, he said he had known all these things for some time, but Pico's words on his sickbed about an apparition of our Lady led him to wonder and worry whether Pico had been deceived by some devilish trickery, since it appeared as if our Lady's promise had been rendered void by his death. Later, however, he came to understand that Pico was deceived by an ambiguous turn of phrase and took what she said about the second, everlasting death to refer to the death that is first and temporal. And later still this same Girolamo told an acquaintance that Pico had appeared to him after death in the midst of flames and told him this was how he was punished in purgatory for his ⌐negligence¬ and lack of gratitude.

⌐Since now he is consigned to that fire from which undoubtedly he will pass unto glory, and since no man can be sure how long he will be in that state—a span of time that may be shortened by our acts of intercession—let all Christians show him charity by helping to speed him on his way.

Having dwelt with those who dwell in this dark world to whom his good conversation gave much light, and having experienced the dark fire of purgatory where venial sins are burned away, may he soon enter—if indeed he has not already—the inaccessible and infinite light of heaven. And there, in the presence of the sovereign Godhead, may he so pray for us that we in turn may be sharers by his intercession in that same ineffable joy to which we have prayed he might speedily be brought. Amen. ¬

⌐Here ends the life of Giovanni Pico, Earl of Mirandola. ¬

CHAPTER TWO

⌐THREE EPISTLES BY PICO DELLA MIRANDOLA,

Two Written to His Nephew, Gianfrancesco, and The Third to Andrea Corneo, an Italian Nobleman⌐

⌐The Argument and Matter of Pico's First Epistle to His Nephew Gianfrancesco.

IT APPEARS FROM THIS LETTER that Gianfrancesco had opened his heart to Pico and consulted him about some secret spiritual matter that he had in mind. But what this was we cannot clearly tell from the letter. In any case, having formed this intention, he encountered many obstacles and circumstances contrary to what he purposed. These to some extent deterred him and held him back. Therefore Pico comforts him in the letter and urges him to persevere, by means evident and clear enough from the letter. Nonetheless, lest you overlook the point—the one in the letter's opening, where Pico says that, unless we are careful, our flesh may become drunk with the cups of Circe and debase us to the likeness and manner of brute beasts—here is how it should be understood.

In Aeaea there once lived a woman named Circe who by enchantment, as Virgil recounts,[1] administered a potion that

---

[1] *Aeneid* 7:15–20.

transformed any men who drank it into the likeness and manner of various beasts—some into lions, some into bears, some into swine, some into wolves; they then walked tamely about her dwelling and did her bidding in whatever she wished.

It is the same with the flesh if it makes us drunk with the wine of voluptuous pleasure or causes the soul to abandon reason's noble use and turn to sensuality and bodily desires: the flesh then changes us from the substance of reasonable men to the likeness of beasts without reason. That happens in various ways, according to the likeness and resemblance between our sensual inclinations and the brutish properties of sundry beasts—the proud-hearted man becoming a lion, the wrathful a bear, the lecherous a goat, the drunken glutton a swine, the ravenous extortioner a wolf, the dishonest deceiver a fox, the mocking jester an ape. Nor may we be restored from our beastly likenesses to our own likeness until such time as we vomit out the wine of corporal lust that first enchanted us in this way.

When some strange beast comes to town, as now and then happens, we run after it and are willing to pay money to have a look; but if men took a good look at themselves, I fear they would see far stranger beasts closer to home. For they would see themselves changed in soul by their wretched inclination to various beastly passions into the forms of not just one but many beasts, namely, all those whose brutish appetites they pursue.

As Pico counsels, let us beware of getting drunk on Circe's cups—on the sensual desires of the flesh, that is—lest we mar God's image in our souls, the image of Him in Whose likeness we have been made, and make ourselves worse than idolaters. For if he is hateful to God who turns a beast's image into his god, how much more hateful he who turns God's image into a beast? ¬

Giovanni Pico, Earl of Mirandola, to Gianfrancesco,
his nephew by his brother:

Good health in Him Who is health itself.

There is no reason, my son, why you should be surprised,
regretful, or disturbed at the many ills which have befallen
you since your leave-taking and which are in conflict with
your good intentions. For how remarkable it would be if to
you alone among all mortal men the way to heaven lay wide
open, without your having so much as to sweat: as if now, for
the first time ever, the deceitful world and the accursed devil
had let you down, and as if you were no longer in the flesh,
which lusts against the spirit and, unless we be on guard and
look carefully to ourselves, will make us drunk on Circe's
cups and change us into the monstrous shapes of brute beasts
that lack reason.

⌐Remember also, when such ills befall you,¬ that the holy
apostle Saint James says you have cause to be glad, writing,
"Be glad, my brothers, when you fall into various trials"[2]—and
not without reason. For what hope of glory is there without
hope of victory, and what opportunity for victory unless there
be battle? He is invited to receive the crown of triumph who
is drawn into the struggle—that struggle in which no one is
overcome against his will and victory requires only the desire
to overcome ourselves. Truly happy is the Christian, since
victory is within grasp of his free will, and victory's reward will
be far greater than we can either hope or imagine.

I pray you tell me, my dear son, what in the end do all
those delights over which earth-bound minds so fret and strain
count for? Is there, I say, any of those trifles that does not
require a man to undergo many labors, many disappointments,
and many miseries before he gets it?

The merchant thinks himself well served if, after ten years
of failure, a thousand setbacks, a thousand life-threatening

---

[2] James 1:2.

scrapes, he may at last have accumulated a bit more than he had at the start. I need write you nothing about courting and serving this world—experience has taught you the wretchedness of that and goes on teaching you every day. What a mountain of dreariness there is in winning the favor of princes, purchasing the friendship of the crowd, and ambitious labor for offices and honors! I could learn more than teach you about what great anguish, business and trouble it is; for, remaining content with my books and my rest, I learned as a child to live at ease with my own situation in life and, dwelling with myself as much as I could, to labor for or desire nothing more.

Take my word for it, scarcely with sweating and groaning shall we obtain the things of this earth, unstable, uncertain, vile, and common as they are both to us and the brute beasts; and do we therefore expect the heavenly things of God (which neither eye has seen nor ear heard nor heart imagined) to drop into our laps, so to speak, while we doze and dream, as if without us God could not reign and the citizens of heaven could not get along?

If it were possible to achieve worldly felicity while staying idle and at ease, then a man who shrinks from hard work might well prefer to serve the world instead of God. But as matters stand, it's as hard to travel the way of sin as the way of God, and indeed even harder ("We are weary of the way of wickedness,"[3] cry the damned); and you would have to be wholly out of your mind not to prefer labor that leads to reward over labor that leads to pain. I pass over what a great source of peace and felicity it is to the mind when a man has nothing troubling on his conscience and is not pricked by the secret goad of hidden evil-doing. This unquestionably is a pleasure that far exceeds all other pleasures that can be obtained or desired in this life.

What deserves desiring among the delights of the world, whose seeking wearies us, whose getting blinds us, whose

---

[3] Wis 5:7.

losing gives us pain? Are you uncertain, my son, whether the minds of wicked men are or aren't troubled with constant fretting and torment? God's word tells us so—that word that can neither deceive nor be deceived: "The wicked man's heart is like a stormy sea that may not rest."[4] Nothing is certain, nothing peaceable, to him; but all things are sorrowful, all deadly. Shall we chase after them and, forgetting our own country, heaven, where we are freeborn children of a heavenly Father, make ourselves their bondsmen, so as, having lived wretchedly with them, still more wretchedly to die and in the end most wretchedly to be punished in everlasting fire? Oh, the darkened minds of men! Oh, their blind hearts! How can anyone fail to see, clearer than clearly, that all this is, as the saying goes, truer than truth? And still we fail to do what we know ought be done. How pointless to lift one foot out of the muck when you stay stuck in it just the same!

Don't doubt it, my son, in familiar surroundings countless obstacles will come your way to keep you from purposing to live well and virtuously, and, unless you're careful, will cast you down head over heels. But the really deadly pestilence of all is spending your days and nights among people who don't just live lives that are an enticement to sin but, still worse, are committed to smothering virtue—under their captain, the devil, under the banner of death, on hell's payroll, warring against our Lord God and His Christ.

Join your voice to the prophet's: "Let us break their bonds and cast off their yoke."[5] These, ⌐as the glorious apostle Saint Paul says,¬ are the ones our Lord has given up to dishonorable and guilty passions to do blameworthy deeds full of iniquity, envy, killing, contention, guile, and malice—to be gossips, hateful to God, insolent, proud, haughty, devisers of evil things, foolish, dissolute, without affection, faithless, merciless.

---

[4] Is 57:20.
[5] Ps 2:3.

Though they see God's justice daily, they fail nonetheless to grasp that people who commit such acts are deserving of death⁶—and not only those who commit them but those who consent to their committing.

And so, my child, don't think to please those who find no pleasure in virtue, but keep constantly before your eyes these words of the apostle: "We must please God rather than men."⁷ And ⌐bear in mind, too, these words of Saint Paul⌐: "If I should please men, I would not be Christ's servant."⁸ Make room in your heart for a holy pride, and scorn to receive as instructors about your manner of life those who have more need to take you as instructor about theirs. Far more seemly would it be that they by joining you in good living should begin to be men, than that you shamefully join them in becoming a beast by abandoning your good resolve.

I tell you by almighty God, sometimes I grow faint and very nearly swoon in wonderment: Just looking at myself, I scarcely know whether to speak of remembering or regretting, marveling at or bewailing, men's cravings—or, to put it bluntly, their craziness. For surely it is great madness to disbelieve the Gospel, whose truth cries out from the blood of martyrs, resounds in the voice of apostles, is exhibited by miracles, confirmed by reason, testified to by the world, declared by the elements, confessed by devils; but still greater madness is it if, not doubting the Gospel's truth, one then lives as if having no doubt that it was false.

For if the Gospel speaks the truth in declaring it extremely difficult for a rich man to enter the kingdom of heaven, why do we daily long to heap up riches? And if it is true that we should seek the glory and praise that come from God rather than men, why do we hang upon men's judgment and opinion,

---

⁶ Cf. Rom 1:26, 28–32.
⁷ Acts 5:29.
⁸ Gal 1:10.

while no one takes any notice whether God approves of him or not? And if we truly believe the time will one day come when God will say either, "Depart from me, you cursed people, into everlasting fire"[9] or else, "Come, you my blessed children, inherit the kingdom that has been prepared for you from the foundation of the world,"[10] why do we fear nothing less than hell and desire nothing less than God's kingdom?

What else is one to conclude except that many are Christians in name but few in deed? But you, my son, force yourself to enter by the strait gate ⌐that leads to heaven,¬ and take no heed of anything man may do but only of what the true law of nature, human reason, and ⌐our Lord Himself¬ tell you should be done. For your glory will not be less if you are happy in company with few, nor will your pain be more easily borne if you are wretched with many.

Against the world and the devil you have two particularly effective remedies with which, as if by two wings, you shall be lifted out of the vale of tears into heaven: almsgiving and prayer. What can we do without God's help, and how is He to help us unless he is besought? Before even that, however, you can be sure He will not hear you when you call upon Him if you do not first hear the poor man when he calls upon you. Surely it is fitting that God should despise you, a man, if you, being such a one, despise a man. For it is written, "In the measure that you give it shall be given to you."[11] And in another place in the Gospel, "Blessed are the merciful, for they shall receive mercy."[12]

When I stir you to pray, I do not mean prayer of many words but that prayer which speaks honestly to God in the secret chamber of the mind and the privy closet of the soul.

---

[9] Mt 25:41.

[10] Mt 25:34.

[11] Mt 7:2.

[12] Mt 5:7.

This is the prayer by which one not only makes oneself present in mind to the Father through the glowing darkness of contemplation but joins one's mind to him in an ineffable manner known only to those who have experienced it. I do not care how long ⌐or short¬ your prayer is, but how effectual, how ardent, and that it be broken and punctuated by sighs rather than drowned in an endless stream of verbosity.

If you are concerned for your well-being, if you wish to be safe from the snares of the devil, the storms of this world, the ambush of your enemies; if you long to be acceptable to God, if you crave to be happy at the last—then let no day pass without at least once making yourself present to God in prayer and, falling flat on the ground before Him filled with the humble sentiments of a devout mind, cry out—not from the surface of your lips but from the inmost reaches of your heart—these words of the prophet: "The offenses of my youth and foolishness remember not, good Lord; but according to Your mercy, Lord, for the sake of Your goodness remember me."[13]

Both the Holy Spirit, who prays on our behalf, and also your own need will tell you hour by hour what to seek from God in your prayer; and you shall also find matter enough for prayer in the reading of Holy Scripture, which I heartily urge you now to keep constantly at hand while setting aside poets, fables, and trifles. You can do nothing more pleasing to God or more profitable to yourself than constantly, day and night, take up and read the books of Holy Scripture. Provided one turns to them with an honest and humble heart, there lies hidden in these pages a certain heavenly strength, lively and effective, with marvelous power to transform the reader's mind and turn it to the love of God.

But now I have gone beyond a letter's length, drawn by my subject and my great love for you, both before and especially since the time I first learned of your holy purpose. In

---

[13] Ps 25 (24):7.

conclusion, then, I warn you (as I often did when we were last together) never to forget these two things: that the Son of God died for you, and that, no matter how long you live, you will in fact die quite soon. With these two thoughts—one fearful, one loving—spur on your steed through the brief journey of this passing life to the reward of eternal felicity. For neither ought we nor may we set ourselves any goal but the endless enjoyment of the infinite good of both soul and body in everlasting peace.

Farewell and fear God.

[From Ferrara, May 15, 1492]

⌐The Matter or Argument of Pico's Letter to Andrea Corneo

This Andrea, a distinguished man and particular friend of Pico's, had advised him in letters to give up studying philosophy, since he thought Pico had spent enough time on that and he judged it vain and unprofitable unless applied to the accomplishment of some real business. He therefore counseled Pico to leave off study and place himself among some of the great princes of Italy, with whom (so Andrea said) he would be occupied much more fruitfully than in forever studying and learning philosophy. Pico's answer, as appears in this present letter, thus means: It would follow from what is said that it was either servile or at least not princely to study philosophy for any reason except a mercenary one—meaning by mercenary all those things we do for pay or reward. Thus he makes philosophy mercenary and treats it as merchandise for those who study it with an eye to what may bring them some material gain or worldly advantage rather than the pleasure it gives ⌐or the instruction of their minds in moral virtue¬.[14]

---

[14] More adds this phrase as part of his summary of the argument that follows, even though Pico does not give this reason in his letter.

Giovanni Pico Earl of Mirandola to Andrea Corneo,

Greetings.

You exhort me by your letters to take up a public and active life, saying I have spent all this time studying philosophy uselessly and, as it were, to my reproach and shame unless I finally put that learning to use by engaging in some profitable activity and tangible business. Indeed, my dear friend Andrea, I would be rid of both the expense and trouble of these studies if I were convinced that in this matter I could find it in my heart to agree with you and take your advice.

This is a very deadly and monstrous notion that has entered into men's thinking, namely, that philosophical studies must either be entirely avoided by lords and princes or, at most, sipped sparingly and tasted lightly, more to polish up and show off their cleverness than to cultivate ⌐and profit¬ their minds. They take as absolute law Neoptolemus's saying that philosophy should be studied either not at all or not for long; but they regard as jokes, indeed as fables, the assertions of wise men that sure and lasting happiness resides only in the goodness of the mind, while outer things of the body or mere happenstance count for little or nothing with us.

But just here you will say to me: ⌐"It's fine with me that you study, but I would have you engaged with the world around you as well.¬ I don't want you to embrace Martha to such an extent that you give up Mary entirely. ⌐Love them and do them both: study and worldly business."¬

⌐Really, my dear friend,¬ on this point I don't deny what you say; nor do I find any fault with, or blame, those who do. But surely it's not the same thing to say that one does well in doing something and that one does evil *unless* one does it. There is a great difference between thinking it acceptable to move downward from contemplation to the active life—⌐from the better to the worse, that is¬—and thinking it wrong to persist in what is better and not take that downward step. Should a man then be rebuked for desiring virtue and pursuing it only for its own sake—because he studies the mysteries of God, because he probes the wisdom of nature, because he makes constant use of pleasant leisure and rest, seeking no outward thing, despising all else, because the things that interest him are quite sufficient to content one who cares about them? By this reckoning it is something servile, or at least not princely, to study wisdom for any reasons but mercenary ones.

Who can hear this, who can abide it? Surely he never studied for wisdom's sake who studied for reasons that rendered him unfit or unwilling to do that in the future. A man acting thus was busy studying merchandise, not wisdom. You write me that the time now has come for me to place myself ⌐in the households of¬ some great princes of Italy, but I perceive that you have not yet grasped how philosophers see themselves. In their eyes, as Horace remarks, they are kings of kings; ⌐they love liberty;¬ they cannot bear the proud manners of people of high rank; they cannot serve. They dwell within themselves and are content with the tranquility of their own minds. Unto themselves they are sufficient, and more than sufficient. They seek nothing outside themselves. Things held in honor among common people are not honorable in their eyes. Whatever men's lustful desires thirst after or ambition seeks they set at naught and despise. And while all this applies to everyone, undoubtedly it pertains especially to those so generously favored by fortune that they can live not only well and prosperously but also nobly.

These great positions raise a man on high and put him on display, but it often happens that they throw down their master as a fierce and skittish horse throws his. Always, certainly, they grieve and vex him, tearing at him rather than bearing him up. What is desirable is the golden mean, ⌐the midpoint,¬ which will more gently shelter us in its hands, obeying us and not playing the master to us.

Standing firmly by this opinion, I therefore attach more importance to my little house, my study, the enjoyment of my books, ⌐the rest¬ and peace of my mind, than to all your kings' palaces, all your public business, ⌐all your glory,¬ all the advantages you are so keen on, and all the favor of the court. Nor do I hope that my studies will result in my being thrust hereafter into the raging torrent of your worldly affairs; but only that I may finally bring forth the offspring I labor upon— bring forth for the common ⌐profit,¬ that is, some books of my own that may contain something of the savor, if not of learning, then at least of intelligence and diligence.

And lest you suppose I've at all neglected or slacked off from my diligent efforts, let me tell you that after much hard work, with a lot of concentration and indefatigable labor, I have learned both the Hebrew and Chaldean tongues, and have now turned my attention to overcoming the great challenge of Arabic. Things like these, my dear friend, I have always thought, and think now, do pertain to a noble prince.

⌐Fare well.¬

Written at Paris,[15] the fifteenth day of October,
in the year of grace 1492[16]

⌐The Argument of the Epistle that Follows

It appears from this letter that after Gianfrancesco, Pico's nephew, had begun to change his manner of living (as we saw from Pico's first letter to him), people at the court where he was well known began making various remarks (as is their unmannerly manner) that, as they supposed, reflected badly on him, but that actually reflected badly on themselves. Some judged it foolishness, some called it hypocrisy, some scorned him, some slandered him. And all this detraction (as we may

---

[15] Thus in the original. A misreading for Perugia.

[16] In fact, the letter was written in 1486.

conclude from the present letter) he shared with Earl Pico, his uncle, who here comforts and encourages him, as can be seen in what follows. ¬

Giovanni Pico, Earl of Mirandola, to his nephew Francesco:

Greetings ⌐in the Lord. ¬

Happy are you, my son, when our Lord not only gives you grace to live well but, while you are living well, gives you grace to bear the evil words spoken ⌐by evil people¬ on that account. Surely there is as much praise in being blamed by the blameworthy as in being commended by the praiseworthy. Nevertheless, ⌐my son, ¬ I don't call you happy because being falsely reproached like this is honorable and glorious to you, but because our Lord Jesus Christ (who isn't merely truthful but is truth itself[17]) affirms that we shall be richly rewarded in heaven when men speak evil to us and, lying, against us.[18] This is an apostle's dignity: to be judged worthy ⌐in God's eyes¬ to be defamed by wicked people for his name.

For we read in the gospel of Luke that the apostles went forth from the council chamber of the Jews joyful and glad because God had found them worthy to suffer wrong and reproof for his sake.[19] Let us therefore rejoice and be glad if we are found worthy before God of the great honor of having his honor made manifest by our being rebuked. And if we suffer anything grievous or bitter at the world's hands, let this sweet saying of our Lord be our consolation: "If the world hates you," ⌐says the Lord, ¬ "know that it hated me before you."[20]

If, then, the world hated Him by whom the world was made, shall we men, vile simpletons that we are—and, if we take a serious look at our wretched way of living, deserving of all

[17] Cf. Jn 14:6.
[18] Cf. Mt 5:11.
[19] The reference is not actually to Luke's gospel but to Acts 5:27–42, also written by St. Luke.
[20] Jn 15:18.

the shame and reproof that come from the backbiting and evil speech of others—be so exercised at the prospect of having evil spoken of us that we start doing it instead? Let us rather receive these evil words gladly, and if we aren't lucky enough to suffer for the sake of virtue and truth, as the saints of old suffered beating, bondage, prison, sword, ⌐and death,¬ let us at least think ourselves well served in having been permitted to suffer the chiding, detraction, and hatred of wicked men, lest, all chance of merit being removed, there be no hope of reward left to us.

If men praise you for your good life, your virtue, insofar as it is virtue, does indeed make you resemble Christ; but insofar as it is praised, it makes you unlike Him, Who was rewarded for His virtue by the ⌐shameful¬ death of the cross for which, as the apostle says, God has exalted him and given Him a name above all names.[21] So it is more desirable to be condemned by the world and exalted by God than to be exalted by the world and condemned by God. The world's condemnation leads to life, and God then exalts to glory; the world's exaltation leads to a fall, and then God condemns to the fire of hell.

If, finally, the world fawns upon you, it may just be that your virtue (which should all be directed upward to the end of pleasing God alone) is to some degree directed to the whispering of sweet nothings to the world and the winning of people's favor. And so, though it take nothing away from our essential perfection, it does nevertheless take something from the reward—a reward which, if we begin to take payment while yet in this world where everything has less value, shall count for less in heaven, where all things are on a grand scale.

O happy rebukes, which give us the certainty that neither shall our virtue wither from the pestilential blasts of vainglory nor our eternal reward be diminished for the worthless puffery of a little vulgar fame! My son, let's love these rebukes and like faithful servants with a holy ambition take pride only in the

---

[21] Cf. Eph 1:21.

ignominy and reproof of our Lord's cross. "We preach Christ crucified," says Saint Paul, "a stumbling block to Jews and folly to Gentiles, but to us the power and wisdom of God."[22] The wisdom of this world is foolishness before God; and the folly of Christ is that by which He has overcome the wisdom of the world and God has been pleased to save those who believe in Him.

If you doubt the madness of those who speak ill of your virtue, taking the Christian way of life—wisdom itself—for madness, think how much greater your madness would be were you, reacting to the judgment of madmen, to turn aside from the good foundation of your life; for all error is to be removed by amendment, not increased by imitation and doing the same thing. So let them neigh, let them bawl, let them bark: go forth boldly on your journey as you've begun, and learn from their wickedness and misery how much you owe God, who enlightened you as you sat in the shadow of death and, removing you from the company of those who wander hither and thither in the dark like drunken men without a guide, made you one with the children of light.

Let our Lord's sweet words sound always in your ears: "Leave dead men with dead men, and you follow me."[23] Truly dead are they who do not live for God and, in the course of this temporal death, go to great trouble to buy themselves eternal death. If you ask where they are heading, to what their studies, their works and their business are directed, and, finally, to what end they devote themselves that would make them happy, either they will have absolutely no answer or they will utter words in themselves repugnant or contradictory, like the raving of people in Bedlam.

Nor do they themselves know what they're doing, but like creatures swimming in swift streams they are borne along by

[22] 1 Cor 1:23–24.
[23] Mt 8:22.

the violence of evil custom just as such creatures might be by a stream's current. Blinded on this side by their wickedness and on that spurred on by the devil, they rush headlong into every sort of misdeed, blind guides of blind men,[24] until without warning death comes upon them and the words ⌐ Christ speaks in the Gospel ¬ are spoken to them: "My friend, this night ⌐ the devils ¬ will have your soul from you."[25] To whom then will all this wealth you've accumulated belong? Then people will envy those they despised, commend those they mocked, crave to model their lives—something no longer possible—on those they harassed rather than heeded.

Therefore stop up your ears, my most dear son, and no matter what men say of you, no matter what men think of you, count it as nothing, but attend only to the judgment of God. He will repay every man according to his own deeds when He comes down from Heaven with the angels of His power, amidst blazing flames, wreaking vengeance on those who have not known God or obeyed His Gospel. They, as the apostle says,[26] in death will suffer eternal pain, from the face of our Lord and from the glory of his power, when He will come to be glorified in His saints and to be made wonderful in all those who have believed. It is written: "Fear not those," says our Lord, "who can kill the body, but those who can cast the soul into Gehenna."[27]

How much less, then, are they to be feared who can harm neither soul nor body? Though they criticize you now, while you live ⌐ virtuously, ¬ they would nevertheless do the same if, having abandoned virtue, you were deeply sunk in vice—not that vice troubles them but that the vice of backbiting always amuses them. Flee for safety's sake if you can, flee as far as possible from their company, and, returning to yourself, pray often

[24] Cf. Mt 15:14.
[25] Cf. Lk 12:20.
[26] Cf. 2 Thess 1:7–10.
[27] Mt 10:28; Lk 12:4.

in secret to the most benign Father ⌐in heaven,¬ crying out with the prophet: "To You, O Lord, I lift up my soul: in You I trust, I shall not be ashamed, even though my enemies mock me. Surely all those who trust in You shall not be ashamed. Let them be ashamed who do wickedness in vain. Your ways, good Lord, show me, and Your paths teach me. Direct me in Your truth, and teach me: for You are God, my Savior; in You shall I trust all the day."[28]

Remember, too, my son, that death is near. Remember that the whole of your life is but a moment or even less. Remember how vicious is that ancient enemy of ours who offers us the kingdoms of this world so that he might deprive us of the kingdom of heaven; how false are those pleasures of the flesh that embrace us in order to strangle us; how deceitful these ⌐worldly¬ honors that lift us up in order to cast us down; how deadly these riches that poison us more the more we sup on them; how short, how uncertain, how much like a shadow, false and imaginary, is all that these things together may bring us even though they come our way just as we would wish.

Remember also what great things are promised to and prepared for those who, despising present things, desire and pine for that country whose king is our Lord God, whose law is charity, whose measure is eternity. Busy your mind with meditating on these things and such others as may awaken you when you sleep, enkindle you when you grow cold, confirm you when you waver, and exhibit the wings of God's love as you struggle heavenward, so that when you come home to us (something we await with great desire), we see not just somebody but the sort of somebody we hope to see.

Farewell, and love God, whom you long ago began to fear.

At Ferrara, the second day of July,
⌐the year of our Redemption,¬ 1492

---

[28] Ps 25 (24): 1–5.

PART TWO

SPIRITUAL COMPENDIUM

GIOVANNI PICO'S COMMENTARY ON THE PSALM "KEEP ME, GOOD LORD"

Psalm 16 [15]

− ¹ Keep me, good Lord,

   ² for I have trusted in You.

   ³ I have said to our Lord: my God are You,

   ⁴ for You have no need of my goods.

   ⁵ To his saints who dwell in His land He has made
      marvelous His will.

  ^{6a} Their infirmities were multiplied,

  ^{6b} and after that they hastened.

   ⁷ I shall not convene their assemblies of blood, nor shall
      I remember their names.

   ⁸ Our Lord is the share of my inheritance.

   ⁹ You, good Lord, are He who shall restore my inheritance
      to me.

  ¹⁰ The cords have fallen out well to me.

  ¹¹ My inheritance is generous in my eyes.

  ¹² I shall bless our Lord, Who has given me understanding.

  ¹³ My reins have troubled me throughout the night.

  ¹⁴ I had God always before my eyes.

  ¹⁵ He is at my right hand, so that I am not moved
      or troubled.

16 My soul is glad,

17 and my flesh will rest in hope.

18 For You will not leave my soul in hell:

19 Nor will You suffer Your holy one to see corruption.

20 You have shown me the ways of life:

21 You will fill me full of gladness with Your cheer.

22 Delight and joy will be at Your right hand forever.[1] ¬

1) "Keep me, good Lord." There is one peril in it if a virtuous man considers his own condition, namely, that he may grow proud of his virtue. Thus David, speaking as a righteous man of his station, begins with the words "Keep me, ¬good Lord¬."

That "Keep me," if well considered, removes any occasion for pride. For he who can get something by himself can keep it by himself. It follows that someone who asks God to preserve him in the state of virtue thereby implies that from the very start he did not acquire his virtue unaided; and he who realizes that he did not attain virtue by his own power but by God's is thereby not proud but instead humbled before God, according to those words of the apostle, "What have you that you have not received?"[2] And if you have received it, why be proud of it as if you hadn't received it?

---

[1] *Conserva me Domine quoniam speravi in te. Dixi Domino: Deus meus es Tu, quoniam bonorum meorum non eges. Sanctis qui sunt in terra ejus mirificavit voluntates suas. Multiplicatae sunt infirmitates eorum postea acceleraverunt. Non congregabo conventicula eorum de sanguinibus: nec memor ero nominum eorum per labia mea. Dominus pars hereditatis meae et calicis mei: tu es qui restitues_hereditatem meam mihi. Funes ceciderunt mihi in praeclaris: etenim hereditasmea praeclara est mihi. Benedicam Dominum qui tribuit mihi intellectum: insuper et usque ad noctem increpuerunt me renes mei. Providebam Dominum in conspectu meo semper, quoniam a dextris est mihi ne commovear. Propter hoc laetatum est cor meum et exultavit lingua mea, insuper et caro mea requiescet in spe. Quoniam non derelniques animam meam in inferno: nec dabis sanctum tuum videre corruptionem. Notas mihi fecisti vias vitae: adimplebis me laetitia cum vultu tuo. Delectationes in dextera tua usque in finem.*

[2] 1 Cor 4:7.

Two sayings, then, we must have ever on our lips: the first—"Have mercy on me, Lord"[3]—when we think upon our vice; the other—"Keep me, good Lord"—when we recall our virtue.

2) "For I have trusted in You." This one thing allows us to obtain what we ask from God: firm hope and trust that we shall be successful. And if ⌐in making our requests¬ we keep two things in mind—to ask for nothing but what is good for us, and to ask for it fervently, with firm hope that God will hear us—our prayers will never be in vain.

Therefore, when we do not get what we ask, it is for one of two reasons. First, we ask for something that would do us harm—as Christ says, we know not what we ask for[4] (but Jesus also said, "Whatsoever you ask in My name, it shall be given you";[5] and this name, Jesus, signifies savior, so that nothing is asked in Jesus' name except ⌐what is wholesome and helpful¬ to the asker's salvation). Second, God does not hear our prayer because, although what we ask for is good, still we do not ask rightly inasmuch as we ask with little hope. He who asks doubtfully asks coldly; and Saint James tells us to ask in faith, without any doubts.[6]

3) "I have said to our Lord: my God are You." Having girded and fenced himself against pride, he now describes his condition in these words. The whole state of a righteous man is summed up in these words: "I have said to our Lord, my God are you." Although these words would appear to apply to everyone, there are ⌐very¬ few who can say them truthfully. A man takes as his god whatever he takes as his chief good; and though he lack everything except what he takes as chief good, he thinks

---

[3] Ps 51 (50):1.
[4] Cf. Mt 20:22.
[5] Jn 14:12.
[6] Cf. Jas 1:6.

himself happy if he has that—while having everything else but lacking that, he thinks himself unhappy.

So the miser says to his money, "My god are you." For although honor fail and health and strength and friends, as long as he has money he considers himself well off. And having all those things, he thinks himself unhappy if the money fails. The glutton says to his physical craving and the ambitious man to his idle glory: "You are my god." See, then, how few can say these words truthfully: "I have said to our Lord, my God are You." For only he can truthfully say that who finds contentment in God alone; so that were he offered all the kingdoms of the world and all the good things on earth and in heaven, he would not offend God even once to have them all. In these words, then, "I have said to our Lord, my God are You," one finds the entire state of a righteous man.

4) "For You have no need of my goods." In these words he shows why he says "My God are You" to our Lord alone. For only our Lord needs no good of ours. There is, as philosophers and theologians show, no creature that doesn't need other creatures, even though they be less perfect than itself: for if these ⌐less perfect creatures¬ didn't exist, neither could those other, ⌐more perfect ones.¬ After all, if any part of the whole universe of creatures were destroyed and no longer existed, the whole of it would be jeopardized. For certainly, if ⌐one part of¬ the universe were to perish, all parts would perish—and of that universe all creatures are parts.

But God is not a part. He is the origin and depends upon nothing. For surely He gained nothing by creating the world, and He would lose nothing if the world were annihilated and returned again to non-being. So God alone is He who has no need of our good. Indeed, we ought surely to be ashamed to take for God some thing that has need of us—and every creature is like that. Moreover, we should not take for God—for the sovereign good of everything, that is—anything except that which is the highest good of all things, and that is not the goodness of any creature. Only to our Lord therefore ought we to say, "My God are you."

5) "To his saints who dwell in his land He has made marvelous his will." After God himself we ought especially to love those nearest to God, as are the holy angels and blessed saints in their heavenly home. Therefore, after saying to our Lord, "My God are You," he adds that our Lord has made wonderful his will: He has made wonderful his love and his desires regarding his saints who dwell in his country, that is, in the country of heaven, which is called the land of God and the land of the living. And certainly, considering how great that country's felicity is and how much the misery of this world, how great the goodness and charity of the ⌐blessed¬ citizens of that land, we desire continually to be quit of this place so that we might be there.

In recalling these and other such things, we should ⌐always¬ be careful to see that our meditations are not fruitless. Rather, in meditating we should always purchase one virtue or another: as, for example, by meditating on the goodness of the heavenly country, acquire the virtue by which, more than just accepting death bravely and patiently when the appointed time comes or it's imposed on us as the price of faith in Christ, we also look forward to it, willingly and gladly, in the desire of leaving this vale of wretchedness so as to reign in the heavenly country with God and his holy saints.

6a) "Their infirmities were multiplied, and 6b) after that they hastened." The prophet says this of wicked men. By infirmities he means idols, and so it is in the Hebrew text. As good folk have only one God whom they worship, so evil folk have many gods and idols; for they serve many sensual pleasures, many vain desires, many and diverse passions. And why do they trouble themselves with all these pleasures? Surely it's because they can find none capable of setting their hearts at rest; and so, ⌐as the prophet says,¬ wicked men go on ⌐endlessly circling the same course.¬

6b) Now after these words ⌐"Their idols were multiplied,"¬ there follows, "After them they hastened"—that is, ⌐after their idols:¬ they rush heedlessly and headlong in pursuit of ⌐passions and animal cravings,¬ without thinking about what they're doing. The lesson is that we should hurry after virtue as speedily as they do after vice, and that we should be no less diligent in serving our Lord than they do to serve their lord the devil.

7) Reflecting on the condition of evil people, the just man firmly resolves—as we, too, should do—that in no way what-soever will he follow their example. And so he says, "I shall not convene their assemblies of blood, nor shall I remember their names."

He says "of blood" both because idolaters were accus-tomed to collect the blood of their sacrifices and perform their rites nearby, and also because the lives of evil men totally abandon reason, ⌐whose seat is entirely in the soul,¬ and fol-low the way of sensuality, whose seat is entirely in the blood. ⌐The prophet says not only that he will not convene their assemblies of blood—that is to say, he will offer no sacrifice to their idols—but also that he will not remember their names— that is, he won't discuss or mention the voluptuous pleasures that, although they can be lawfully enjoyed, are the gods of evil people. ¬ In this way he shows us that a perfect man should abstain not only from unlawful pleasures but from lawful ones, so that his mind may be directed wholly heaven-ward and he may the more purely pursue the contemplation of heavenly things.

8) And since someone might perhaps think it foolish for a man to deprive himself entirely of all pleasures, the prophet there-fore adds: "Our Lord is the share of my inheritance"—as if to say, "Do not marvel if I give up everything for the sake of pos-sessing God in whose possession everything else is possessed." Here is something every good Christian ought to say: "God is

the share of my inheritance." For we Christians, to whom God is promised as an inheritance, ought ⌐ surely ¬ to be ashamed at desiring anything but Him.

9) But since it might perhaps be thought highly presumptuous for a man to promise himself God as his inheritance, the prophet therefore addresses God: "You, good Lord, are He who shall restore my inheritance to me," as if to say, "O good Lord, my God, I am well aware that next to You I am nothing, I know well that by my own strength I cannot rise so high as to possess You; but You are the One who will draw me to Yourself by Your grace, You are the One who will give Himself to be possessed by me." Let a righteous man therefore consider what great felicity it is to have God come to him as his inheritance.

10) Next we read ⌐ in the psalm ¬: "The cords have fallen out well to me." In olden times, portions and shares ⌐ of inheritances ¬ were allotted and divided by cords ⌐ or ropes. ¬ To say, then, "The cords have fallen out well to me" is equivalent to saying: my share or portion of the inheritance is a noble one.

11) But there are many men who, though called to this great felicity—as indeed are all Christian people—nevertheless set little store by it and frequently exchange it for some small, trivial delight. This apparently moves the prophet to say, "My inheritance is noble in my eyes." In effect, he is saying, "As it is noble in itself, so also it is noble in my eyes," in other words, "⌐I regard it as noble,¬ and, judged in its light, I regard all else—as Saint Paul puts it [7]—as dung."

12) But inasmuch as this light of understanding enables a man to recognize God's gift to him for what it is—God's gift—the prophet therefore says next: "I shall bless our Lord, Who has given me understanding." For although after thinking it over, a man may decide to serve God, it nevertheless often happens

---

[7] Cf. Phil 3:8.

that the stirrings of the flesh put up resistance; thus a man is perfect only when not just the soul but the flesh, too, draws toward God, ⌐according to the prophet's words in another psalm¬: "My mind and my flesh have both rejoiced in the living God."[8]

13) And then the prophet says: "My reins ⌐(or kidneys)¬ have troubled me throughout the night." In other words: My reins, in which the principal inclination to concupiscence is ordinarily found, not only incline me not to sin but also chide me—draw me away from sin during the night, withdraw me from sin to such an extent that they readily afflict my body and cause it pain. ⌐In Scripture,¬ "night" often signifies affliction, ⌐because it is the time most plagued by ills.¬

14-15) Next the prophet points to the source of this removal, ⌐this deliverance from man's concupiscence of the flesh¬: "I had God always before my eyes." For supposing a man to have God always before his eyes as his master in all he did, and in all of it to seek neither his own profit, glory, or pleasure but only God's, that man would in short order be perfect. And since he who does thus prospers in everything, it therefore follows, "He is at my right hand, so that I am not moved or troubled."

16-19) Then the prophet declares how great is the felicity of the just man, who shall forever be blessed in both body and soul; and so he says: "My soul is glad," knowing that after he dies heaven awaits him. "And my flesh will rest in hope," that is, although it does not rejoice at once, as it would if it were to receive its ⌐glorified¬ state immediately after death, nevertheless it rests in the grave with this hope: that it will rise with his soul immortal and shining on Judgment Day. Indeed, the prophet says this more specifically in the verse that follows, for having said, "My soul is glad," he points to the reason: "For You will not leave my soul in hell." Also, where the prophet

---

[8] Ps 84 (83): 2.

says his flesh will rest in hope, he explains why: "Nor will You suffer Your holy one to see corruption," ⌐that is, "You will not allow the flesh of a good man to become corrupt."¬ For that which was corruptible will rise incorruptible.[9]

And because Christ was first to enter paradise and open to us the way to life—first, too, to rise again and cause of our resurrection—therefore these words spoken of the resurrection are understood principally of Christ, as Saint Peter the apostle has said; and secondarily they may be understood of us, the members of that Christ who alone has never seen corruption inasmuch as His body did not experience decay in the tomb.

20–22) Since, then, the way of a good life leads us to the eternal life of soul and body, the prophet says, "You have shown me the ways of life." And because all felicity of life consists in seeing God plainly and being fulfilled in Him, we next find, "You will fill me full of gladness with Your cheer." And since our felicity will be everlasting, therefore he says, "Delight and joy will be at Your right hand forever"—"at Your right hand" because our felicity is complete in the vision and enjoyment of the humanity of Christ, who in heaven sits at the right hand of ⌐his Father's¬ majesty, as Saint John says, "This is all our reward, that we may behold God and Jesus Christ Whom You have sent":[10] ⌐to which reward may He bring us Who reigns there and prays for us. Amen.¬

---

[9] Cf. 1 Cor 15:53.
[10] Jn 17:3.

CHAPTER FOUR

TWELVE RULES OF GIOVANNI PICO EARL OF MIRANDOLA,

Partly Encouraging and Partly Directing a Man in the Spiritual Struggle

If we refuse the way of virtue because it is painful, we ought for the same reason to refuse the way of sin.

The First Rule

Let him who deems the way to virtue hard
Because we must engage in constant war
Against the world, the flesh, the devil—⌐those
Who ever strive to make us bond and thrall ¬—
Bear it in mind that any path he choose,
Indeed the world's own way, will still give rise
To sorrow, setback, labor, grief, and pain.

The Second Rule

Among the sorrows of this wretched world,
Know that the battle's longer and more fierce,
More burdensome and showing less result,
In which the end of work is naught but work,
⌐And, when the world has left us at the last
Bereft of virtue, our reward in death
Is everlasting pain amid the flames. ¬

The Third Rule

Consider ⌐well¬ the silly ⌐vanity¬
Of seeking heav'n ⌐with pleasure and delight¬
Since Christ, our ⌐Lord and sovereign¬ captain,
Ascended there by bravely bearing arms
And suffering bitter wounds. The point, you'll see,
Is that a servant cannot rightly look
For better treatment than his Lord received.

The Fourth Rule

Think, then, we ought not merely not resent
This strife but should be ⌐glad and joyful¬ of it—
Indeed should crave it (though we cannot see
How any ⌐profit¬ thereby will redound
To us) and in it should ⌐delight¬ to be
Conformed ⌐and like in some behavior¬ to
Our blessed Lord and Savior Jesus Christ.

So often, then, as you do fight and strive,
Against your senses' sin-ward inclination,
Some evil prompting stoutly to resist,
With ⌐good devotion¬ may you call to mind
How you resemble Christ; and as you taste
Your cup of bitter pain, think then upon
How Christ drank vinegar and gall for you.

If you hold back your hands and do refrain
From greedy snatching at some thing, think you
How to the cross nails fixed His ⌐innocent¬ hands.
If pride be your temptation, think how He,
Though in the very form of God, yet for
You came a humble servant, suffering death
⌐Most hateful and most vile¬ upon a tree.[1]

---

[1] Cf. Phil 2:6–8.

When moved to wrath, recall to memory
That He Who both was God and best of men,
When treated basely with contempt, and scourged
And thrust as if a thief between two thieves
With much rebuke and shame, still did not speak
The slightest word of anger or of scorn
But all the pain did patiently endure.

If in this vein you thus regard the snares
And clever wiles our devilish foe contrives,
None will you find so evil and accursed
But ⌐you can turn it to a virtuous end.
For by your brave resistance to the fiend,
Your warding off his subtle, fiery dart,¬
Your likeness to our Savior Christ does grow.

The Fifth Rule

Remember well that we are not allowed
To place our trust in armoring the soul
Or remedy of any other sort,
But only in the virtue of our Savior.
For it is He who by His mighty power
The world has conquered and cast out its prince
Who until then had reigned throughout the earth.

In Him let's trust to overcome all evil,
In Him let's place our hope and confidence
To subjugate the flesh and master Satan.
To Him all honor be and reverence.
Oh, let us with all diligence beseech
Him with prayers, with tears, with heartfelt groans
For help of grace and of His holy saints.

The Sixth Rule

With one sin mastered, ⌐do not drop your guard,¬
But be alert another to repel,
For like a raging lion roams the fiend
Abroad in search of whom he may consume;
In constant watch upon your tower, then,
Stand with the prophet vigilant, on guard,
Lest Satan find you unprepared and slack.

The Seventh Rule

Compel yourself, I pray, not just to stand
Unvanquished by the devil's power but,
Still more than that, most valiantly to strive
To vanquish him and drive him from the field.
How done? By making that same deed or thought
Or look by which he'd gladly had you sin
Occasion of a good and ⌐virtuous¬ act.

At times, to stir you unto pride, he subtly
Turns your thoughts upon some glorious deed—
Vainglory blinds a multitude of men.
But make humility your trusty guide,
And praise God as the author of the good
You do. Think it not yours but rather gift
Of Him whose gift all goodness truly is.

The Eighth Rule

Conduct yourself with valor in the fight
That having won the victory you may
Rest happy in a peace that does not end:
For ⌐in His goodness and great mercy¬ God
May grant that gift, while our proud enemy,
Confounded ⌐and confuted¬ by your fight,
Ashamed may be to challenge you again.

Yet even so, when once you've won a triumph,
Prepare yourself and gird for war anew,
As if to sally forth to fight again.
If you're prepared, then will the devils fear you.
And for this reason so comport yourself
As ever to recall and bear in mind:
First must he fight who would the victor be.

The Ninth Rule

If you regard yourself as armed and safe
⌐Against the subtle lure of vice, recall
How fragile glass oft shatters under pressure,
How adventurers do often curse their risks:
If you be wise, then wager modestly, ¬
At all times shun the realms of sin, for he
Who peril loves is sure therein to perish.

The Tenth Rule

When you are tempted, fight back from the start.
⌐How hazardous a thing it is to feed ¬
The cursed brats of wretched Babylon!
Dash out their brains upon a rock instead.[2]
⌐Perilous is the rot that roots itself
In bone, ¬ too late is salve to cure the sore
Allowed to spread and fester by neglect.

The Eleventh Rule

Although in time of battle and of war
The conflict may seem bitter, fierce, and sharp,
Consider how much greater joy will lie
In conquering the evil one, your foe,

---

[2] Cf. Ps 137 (136):9.

Than in any beastly pleasure you may have.
For conscience draws more inner joy from virtue
Than does the body draw from any sin.

Yea, many err in this ⌐by negligence¬:
They fail to measure victory's joy against
The satisfying of their fleshly lusts
And unadvisedly, like untamed beasts
That lack discretion, foolishly do weigh
The gross delight that comes from their foul sin
Against the painful toil of war and strife.

But he, alas, who from experience
Knows all too well what bitter grief it is
To lose in combat to his enemy,
At least for once should exercise himself
By making a determined stand to learn
What pleasure, honor, peace, and rest do come
With glorious victory, triumph, and conquest.

The Twelfth Rule

Though you be tempted, have no thought of quitting.
Instead, think of the glorious apostle Paul,
Whose flesh, when he'd seen God in his perfection—
Lest vanity should then invade his heart—
Was granted leave to rise against his soul.
And so almighty God in His great kindness
Did guard His servant from the threat of pride.

Now here take heed: that he whom God did love
And singled out as his most special tool—
Transporting him to that third heaven on high—
In peril yet did stand from mighty pride.
Well, then, ought we our hearts to rampart round
Against vainglory, ⌐very mother of sin,
And very seed¬ and root of evil fruit.

Against this ⌐empty pomp and worldly luster,¬
Give thought how Christ ⌐the Lord, the sovereign power,¬
For us did humble Himself unto the cross.
Consider, too, how death in time will quickly
Separate us from our wealth and honor,
And turn us, ⌐whether we be small or great,¬
To vile carrion and wretched meat of worms.

CHAPTER FIVE

THE TWELVE WEAPONS OF SPIRITUAL BATTLE,

Which Every Man Should Have at Hand when ⌐The Pleasure¬ of a Sinful Temptation Comes to Mind

- The pleasure scant and brief
- Its companions: grief and weariness
- The loss of something better
- This life itself a dream, a shadow
- Death near at hand and unannounced
- The fear of going forth impenitent
- Eternal ⌐joy¬, eternal pain
- The nature and the dignity of man
- The peace of a good mind
- The ⌐great¬ benefits that come from God
- The ⌐painful¬ cross of Christ
- The witness of martyrs and example of saints

These Twelve Weapons We More Closely Examine as Follows.

The Pleasure Scant and Brief

Think well upon the pleasure you delight in,
No matter whether touch or wanton look,
The daintiest of scents or greedy taste,
Or pleasure whatsoever it may be

That captivates your wretched appetite:
Look at it squarely and you're sure to see
It's little, simple, short, and quickly past.

Its Companions: Grief and Weariness

When good work is rewarded with good fruit,
The fruit will last, the toil will pass away.
But if you pleasure draw from evil deeds,
The pleasure that came partnered with the evil
Slips rapidly away, nor may you keep it;
While yet the evil, lodged within your breast,
Will breed a weary heart and grieving mind.

The Loss of Something Better

When you do sally forth to purchase pleasure,
Be sure you've reckoned on the final cost:
For thus you sell your soul in days to come
To those who are your cruelest enemies.
O mad the merchant, foolish merchandise,
O foolish reckoning that for a trifle
Would pay the dearest treasure we possess!

This Life Itself a Dream, a Shadow

Emboldened by the trust and confidence
That wretched life goes on and on, we sin.
Yet all experience should make it clear
That from its earliest hour life pursues
A steady and unceasing onward course
On which it ever rushes toward its end
As dreams or shadows on a wall do pass.

Death Near at Hand and Unannounced

Be well aware that ever, night and day,
While busily we are engaged in tending
To games and revels, to our mirth and play,
To pleasing melodies, to dainty fare—
Death steals upon us slyly and unseen.
Close by he crouches, ready to attack,
How soon and in what manner know we not.

The Fear of Going Forth Impenitent

If you should give offense to God, think how
Your state at once would be most perilous.
You might have scarce an hour left for cleansing
Sin; and even though that's time enough,
You might perhaps be lacking grace for it.
How fearful to offend, then, ought we be,
Lest from this life impenitent we go!

Eternal Reward, Eternal Pain

You see this world is but a thoroughfare.
Take care, then, to act wisely toward your host;
Since naked and unclothed you will go hence,
Attend unto which realm you will depart,
For when it's time for you to shed
The bondage of this wretched carcass, know
That, joy or pain, forever it will last.

The Nature and the Dignity of Man

Think on it: God gave you reason, made
You very image and resemblance of
Himself, and for you suffered dreadful pain

That for an angel He would ne'er endure.
So think, O man, how high your nature is,
And, made to be a very angel's equal,
Do not for shame become the devil's slave.

The Peace of a Good Mind

Why dote so on these transient, worldly joys?
Take all the mirth, take all the fantasies,
Take all the games and all the fanciful toys,
Take every kind of sport that men devise—
Then take it as a certainty that, 'mongst all,
No pleasure will you find that can compare
With the gladness of a virtuous mind at peace.

The ⌐Great¬ Benefits that Come from God

Besides God's having formed and bought you,
He's richly showered you with benefits.
Though often you have merited His wrath,
Yet has He kept you sheltered up to now,
And daily summons you unto His bliss.
How can you then be loveless unto Him
Who ever unto you has shown such love?

The ⌐Painful¬ Cross of Christ

When temptation blazes in you like flame,
Think then upon the dolorous pain of Christ.
Think of the Man of Sorrows, His piteous cross,
The blood so freely flowing from His veins,
Think of His precious heart now carved in two.
Think how all this He suffered to redeem you.
Let Him not lose you whom He's bought so dear.

The Witness of Martyrs and Example of Saints

Don't say you lack the strength to fight off sin.
It's folly to adopt this poor excuse.
Saints' witness and the martyrs' constancy
Accuse you of a slothful cowardice.
You'll have God's help if you do not refuse,
And if others have resisted, so can you.
For what's once done can be done yet again.

CHAPTER SIX

THE TWELVE PROPERTIES
⌐OR CONDITIONS⌐ OF A LOVER

- To love but one and despise all others for that one
- To think himself unhappy who is not with his love
- To adorn himself for the pleasure of his love
- To suffer anything, even death, to be with his love
- To desire also to suffer harm for the sake of his love, and to consider that injury sweet
- To be always with his love, however he may—if not in fact, then in thought
- To love everything that concerns his love
- To desire that his love be praised and not to tolerate any criticism
- To believe of his love all that is excellent, and to desire that everyone should think the same
- To weep often for the sake of his love: in joy when his love is present, in sorrow when his love is absent
- Always to languish and burn with desire for his love
- To serve his love without thinking of any reward or profit

⌐ *These twelve marks or properties are more fully and clearly expressed in the verses that follow.*[1]

---

[1] This entire section, until the concluding two stanzas, is wholly More's addition.

The First Property

To love but one is first of our twelve marks,
And for that one all others set aside,
For he loves none who gives his love to many.
A mighty flood that flows in many channels
In each of them does run a feeble stream;
So love that's portioned out among too many
Is scarce enough for any single one.

Let you, then, who do say that you love God
Imprint this deeply on your memory:
As He is singular in sovereign worth,
So loves He not divided hearts.
Love Him instead with all He's given you—
For He will not have body, soul, or mind
By parts but only all for Him or naught.

The Second Property

So glad and pleasant to a lover be
The sight and presence of the one he loves
That he whom fortune favors with them both
Believes himself possessed of perfect bliss;
While he who sadly finds himself deprived,
Though rich and easy he be otherwise,
Believes himself unhappy and accursed.

So should God's lover think of one possessed
Of all the pleasure, merriness, and mirth
Which in this world a man can ever have:
That, till time comes when finally he dwells
Amid the blessings of the heavenly home
Where he can look upon God's glorious face,
He knows not perfect joy and true delight.

The Third Property

Third point among a perfect lover's marks
Is taking care that in all things he be
Attractively turned out, no wise unseemly,
But comely, proper, excellent, and clean—
In short, that in himself there shall be naught
Of speech, of dress, of gesture, look or bearing
That gives offense or lessens any charm.

So also you who wish to win God's favor:
Take care, present yourself with such good taste
As elegance dictates, and mannerly
As well conduct yourself. Yet realize
My meaning's not that you should waste your time
On gazing in a glass, but pass your days
In virtuous adorning of your soul.

The Fourth Property

Wherever love is fervent, strong, and warm,
No trouble, grief, or sorrow seems so great
But that the lover would be well content
To bear it all—indeed to think that death
Itself were small, if only he might thus
Obtain the joyful presence of the one
Upon whom he his heart and love has set.

And so with God: God's lover should be pleased
To suffer any sorrow or distress
Than separated from Him he should be.
Indeed, to die he should be pleased, if sure
That passing hence would transport him at last
From this dark valley to the heavenly light
By which he'll gaze upon the One he loves.

The Fifth Property

A lover is not merely glad at heart
But truly yearns and longs that he might have
Some labor, inconvenience, or hurt,
Some loss, some setback, trouble, grief, or pain:
And joyous is he suffering that—yes, glad,
And thinks himself well pleased that he should have
This misadventure for his lover's sake.

And so too also you who do love God
Should long and crave, and in your heart be glad
At suffering trouble, pain, and woe for Him.
Though for Him sore beset perhaps you be,
Ne'er shall you suffer, friend—don't be afraid—
So much as half the sorrow, grief, and pain
That for you He has suffered before now.

The Sixth Property

The perfect lover ever longs to be
In presence of his love both day and night.
And if by chance it so befall that he
Cannot be as he would, yet will he find
Some way of being with his loved one—
If not by presence of his fleshly body,
Then present in his mind and in his thought.

So should God's lover also strive to do
As far as it be in him, even though
He fail to have the company of God
In just that living manner that he'd like.
For though the world cast obstacles his way,
Still he whose body's riveted to earth
Can yet his mind raise heavenward to Him.

The Seventh Property

There is no page or servant, great or small,
Who tenderly upon his love attends—
There is no beast nor simple creature—
That does not cherish the least merest trifle,
A scrap of lace perhaps, a well-worn glove,
And hold it in esteem and dear if it
Some time has passed close to the one he loves.

So let God's lover careful be to keep
All images in reverence and respect,
All relics, too, that speak His radiant glory,
And most especially to honor them
Who on our altars daily make Him present:
Those living icons, priests of holy Church.

The Eighth Property

Above all things on earth the perfect lover
Unceasingly does wish and long to hear
All things that do give rise to praise and honor—
Indeed, that spread the fame both far and wide—
Of his dear love. No wise can he endure
To hear some other tune that would o'erride
Or contradict such melody as this.

So also ought God's lover always wish
To hear the honor, worship, laud, and praise
Of Him Whose goodness none can fully tell,
Whom hell and earth and heaven above obey.
And never should God's perfect lover suffer
The cursed words of blasphemy to pass
Nor aught irreverent of God be said.

The Ninth Property

The perfect lover has no slightest doubt
About the one his heart is set upon:
He's sure that in his love no one will find
Aught other than what's worthy, excellent,
And fair, surpassing far in his esteem
All others he has known by sight or name;
And would that all would think as he!

And so of God, most wonderful and high:
His lover ought in all things value Him,
Ought honor Him—adore, give glory, praise—
That everything created in this world
May shrink to nothing by comparison;
And gladdened ought God's lover be to learn
Some way to make the whole world share his mind.

The Tenth Property

A lover's countenance is deathly pale,
His sleepless eyes do smolder in his head,
No stomach does he have for meat or wine,
And what men say of him he reckons not.
Eat, drink, lie down, sit up, or walk are all
The same, for like a fire in his heart
Desire's flames are raging in his breast.

See here a model also for God's lover:
To keep God constantly in mind,
To meditate on Him and ever pray,
While others play and revel, sing and dance.
No earthly joy, pastime, or foolish sport
Should coax or turn aside his ardent mind
From dwelling upon God, his heavenly love.

The Eleventh Property

A lover's heart is swept by winds of passion:
Now easeful hope, now dread and grievous fear,
Now perfect bliss, now bitter sorrow's sting.
And be the loved one near or far away,
Oft will the tears come coursing from his eyes—
For perfect joy when they two be together,
For pain and sorrow when they be apart.

Like feelings stirred by prayer and meditation
Well up within the breast of one who loves
The Lord: for when in loving contemplation
His happiness o'erflows, then too do spring
The happy tears of joy and fond delight;
And when his Love does purpose to depart, at length does
   leave him,
Again he weeps, though now for pain and woe.

The Twelfth Property

The perfect lover will his love obey.
His joy it is and his desire fulfilled
To put himself to pain what way he must
In serving, day and night with diligence,
That one on whom his tender heart is set
For love alone, not giving any thought
To profit or requital or reward.

So also you whose heart is upward turned
Unto our God: take care that you exert
Yourself with diligence, so no least thing
Distract you ever from His faithful service.
And see that you do render service freely,
Not bound to Him by hope of gain, but by
A faithful heart and loving mind alone. ¬

Three things may lead a man to serve unpaid:
First that he find the work itself reward;
The second that the ones he serves and loves
Be very lovable and good themselves;
Third, ⌐that 'tis only reasonable for us—
With no repining or resentment, mind you—¬
To serve those who have first done us great good.

Serve God for love, then, not for hope of pay.
What happier service could you ever wish
Than service whose performance is your good?
And who so kind, so lovely as is He
Who such great things e'er now for you has done—
First making you, and then upon the cross
Redeeming you with His own precious blood?

CHAPTER SEVEN

A Prayer of Pico Della Mirandola to God

O holy God of awesome majesty,
God truly one in three and three in one,
The angels' Lord and Maker of all things,
Sole Ruler of this earth and heaven above:
We ask You, Lord, and humbly do entreat
That You forgive us wretches, wash our guilt,
And turn away from us Your righteous wrath.

In truth, if You should strictly weigh our sins
On unforgiving scales of rigorous justice,
Who'd hope then to escape Your punishment?[1]
Indeed the fabric of this world, ⌐I say, ¬
Created though it be to last forever,
Could not itself withstand ⌐such scrutiny¬
⌐A single moment in¬ your wrathful hand.

What man among us does not bear old Adam's
Sin and has not added to its sum?
Yet You, our dearest Lord, are all-forgiving,
Your justice ever tempering with mercy.
Thus as You do prepare us for reward
That far exceeds what we deserve, so too
Far less to punish us you kindly choose.

How much beyond our sins God's bounteous mercy!
More godly is it, ⌐and more mercy is there,¬

---

[1] Cf. Ps 130 (129):3.

His gifts upon the unworthy to bestow.
And of sufficient worth He freely makes us,
Though truly worthless we be otherwise,
Whose restoration He has kindly granted:
The formerly ungraced restored to grace.

And so it is, ⌐Lord ever merciful,
We sorry wretches turn with humble hearts
For succor to Your grace and sovereign might:
Look not upon our sins and evil hearts, ¬
But on us gaze, we pray, with kindly eyes,
For whether we be saints or sinners, still
Your creatures are we and we shall remain.

Yea, sinners are we truly, if You choose
Our fickle hearts unruly to regard;
And yet if You instead do choose to see
Your noble gifts again at work in us,
Then truly shall You find us still to be
That which we are and have been from the start—
I mean by nature servants, yours by grace.

And yet Your very goodness testifies
Against us; sin having made us who
By grace were yours into a guilty race,
For weary centuries sunk in that estate.
So pray we, God, that Your abounding grace
Will now unloose us from our evil bondage,
Your glory magnify in conquering sin.

For though Your wisdom and Your sovereign power
To some may seem sufficiently proclaimed,
Since creatures every moment by existing
Declare them loudly with dumb eloquence,
Yet naught gives voice to them so clearly as
Your goodness, bounteous mercy, tender heart—
A Father's pardon of our erring ways.

What else but mankind's sin had been occasion
To show this mighty love? For having drawn to earth
Your awesome majesty, sin then did place
E'en God upon a cross. And thus we wretches
Were truly washed all clean from filthy sin
By blood and water streaming from Your side
And from the blessed wounds of nails and lance.

And so, O heavenly King, Your love and pity
Find matter for Your kindness in our evil.
O love, O pity, riches granting us!
O goodness, that does serve Your servants
⌐In their distress¬! O love, O pity, that
So far exceed our scanty gratitude!
O goodness, ⌐mighty, ever gracious, wise,¬
Which yet our evil nearly overcame!

I pray You pour into my heart such warmth
As may be equal to this love of Yours,
And grant me Satan's bondage to escape
Whom so long serving I do now regret.
I ask you, ⌐kindly Lord, all things' Creator,¬
To quench in me each flame of sinful lust
And set Your love ablaze within my heart.

Then, when this lifelong journeying to death
Has ended for my foolish soul and he
⌐Without his fleshly wife¬ at last must go
Into the presence of his august Lord,
May he, ⌐O well of gracious pardon, in
Your very lordship¬ find not lord but One
Who to him is ⌐a tender, loving¬ father. ⌐Amen. ¬

INDEX

active life, xix–xxi, 35
Adam, 22, 74
Alexander VI, Pope, 10, 10n10
almsgiving, 15–16, 23, 24, 25, 32
Ambrose, St., 6–7
angels, 49, 74
Apollonius, 8, 20
apostles, 31, 38
Aquinas, St. Thomas, 12
Ars Poetica (Horace), xxi–xxii
ascetical life, xii

Babylon, 58
Bedlam, 40
Benivieni, Girolamo, 15–16
Bible, xix, 18
bodily desires, 26–30, 50–53, 59

cabala, xiv, 9n8
canon law, xii, 7–8
Carthusians, xii
Charles, King of France, 23
Christ, 3–4, 11, 14, 21, 30, 31,
    47, 52
  cross of, ix, x, 34, 39–40, 55,
    60, 61, 64, 76
  faith in, 49
  Gospel and, 41
  love of, 21
  Passion of, 16
  resembling, 39, 55
  spiritual battle and, ix–x, 55
  virtue and, 56

Christians, 3–4, 28, 32, 40, 50, 51
Church, xix, 7, 10, 12, 14, 16,
    18, 69
Circe, 26–27, 28
Colet, John, vii, viii, xii, xiv
"Commentary on Psalm 16"
    (Pico), x–xi, xviii, 45–53
concupiscence, 52
conscience, x, xxi, 29, 59
Constantine, Emperor, 4
contemplative life, xix–xxi, 35, 50
Cross of Christ, ix, x, 34, 39–40,
    55, 60, 61, 64, 76
crucifix, 21–22

David, 46
death, 22–23, 30, 31, 39, 41, 42,
    54, 61, 63
De Ente et Uno, 18
devil, x, 28, 30, 33, 41, 50, 57,
    58–59
devotion, ix, 18–19, 21, 55
Dominicans, 13
Donne, John, xix
duty, xx, xxi

Epicurus, 14
Erasmus, xiin2
Ercole d'Este, Duke of Ferrara, 13
excommunication, 10n10

faith, vii, 49

Fathers of the Church, 12
felicity. *See* happiness
Florence, Italy, xiv, 23
Frederick III, Holy Roman
     Emperor, 6
free will, 28
Friars Preacher. *See* Dominicans
friendship, 19–20, 29
     gifts and, 3–4
     with God, ix
     virtue and, xvi

Gehenna, 41
Gentiles, 40
Girolamo, Friar, 23–26
gluttony, 48
God, xv, xxi, 6, 27, 29, 30, 40
     benefits that come from, 61,
          64
     friendship with, ix
     goodness of, 16, 57, 75
     as inheritance, 45, 50–51
     kingdom of, 32
     love of, ix, x, xvi–xvii, xix, 4,
          8, 16, 18, 20–21, 66–73,
          69
     mercy of, 32, 47, 57, 74, 75
     perfection of, 59
     prayer to, 32–33
     trust in, 45, 47
     will of, 49
     word of, 30
Gospel, 31, 32
grace, ix, 15, 34, 38, 74, 75
grief and weariness, 61, 62
Grocyn, William, viii, xiv

happiness, x–xi, xiii, 4, 13, 29,
     34, 49, 51, 72
Heaven, 4, 22, 28, 30, 32, 55
Hell, vii, 30, 39, 46

heresy, xiii, 9–10
Holy Spirit, 33
honor, 5, 17
Horace, xx, 20, 36
human nature, 61, 63–64
humility, x, xvii–xviii, xix, 17–18,
     57

idolatry, idols, xviii, 49–50
Innocent VIII, Pope, 10n10
irony, xv
Italian Renaissance, viii

James, St., 28, 47
Jerome, St., 16
Jesus Christ. *See* Christ
Jews, 38, 40
John, St., 23, 52
joy, ix, x, 58, 59, 61, 63
Judgment Day, 52

"Letter to Corneo" (Pico),
     xix–xx, 34–37
"Letter to Gianfrancesco" (Pico),
     26–34, 37–42
"Letter to Gonell" (Pico), xxi
liberality, 19
liberty, xiii, xvii, xxi, xxn5, 36
The Life of Pico Della Mirandola
     (More), vii, viii–xi, xii
     active-contemplative life and,
          xix–xxi
     engagement of the reader in,
          xxi–xxii
     focus of, xiii, xv–xix
     omissions from, xiv
     puzzle of, viii–xi
     virtue and, xiii–xiv
Linacre, Thomas, viii
love, 3

of Christ, 21
of God, ix, x, xvi–xvii, xix, 4,
   8, 16, 18, 20–21, 66–73,
   69
lover, properties of perfect
   and, ix, xvi, 66–73
Luke, St., xxi, 38

man, dignity of, 61, 63–64
marriage, viii, xiii, 20
Martha, xxi, 35
martyrs, 61, 65
Mary, xxi, 22, 35
Medici, Giuliano dei, xiii
Medici, Margherita dei, xiii, xiv
mercy, 32, 47, 57, 74
miracles, 31
More, Cresacre, viii
More, John, xii
More, Sir Thomas
   active-contemplative life and,
      xix–xxi
   character of, vii
   education of, xii, xiin2
   *The Life of Pico Della
      Mirandola* and, vii–xxii
   Pico della Mirandola, Gio-
      vanni and, viii
   poetry of, ix, xvi
   prayer and, vii
   sense of humor of, vii
   spiritual battle, rules and
      weapons of and, vii
   virtue and, vii
   vocation of, vii, viii
   youth of, xi–xii

negligence, 19, 59
Neoplatonism, xvi
Neoptolemus, 35
900 Theses (Pico), 9–10

nobility, xvi

obedience, xvii, xviii, xix, 36, 41,
   70, 72
Orpheus, 8

pain, 61, 63
Paul, St., 30, 31, 40, 51, 59
Paulinus, 6
peace, ix, x, 29, 61, 64
perfect lover, qualities of, xvi–xvii
perseverance, 26
Peter, St., 52
Petrarch, xvi
philosophy, xx–xxi, 8, 14, 20,
   34–37
Pico della Mirandola, Gianfrancesco, viii, xiii–xiv, xvii, xix,
   21
   letters to, 26–34, 37–42
Pico della Mirandola, Giovanni
   almsgiving of, 15–16
   ancestry of, 11
   appearance of, 7, 11
   birth of, 6–7
   character of, xiii–xiv, 16–20
   death of, xiii, xv, 21–23
   disputations at Rome of, 8–10
   heresy and, xiii, 9–10
   imprisonment of, xiii
   learning of, xii–xiii, 3, 4, 7–8,
      12–13, 14, 18–19
   life of, 3–26
   More, Sir Thomas and, viii,
      4–5
   prayer and, xvi, 15
   state of soul of, 23–26
   virtue and, xiii–xiv, 3, 4, 5,
      11–12, 15
   vocation of, viii, 24
   youth of, xii–xiii

"Pico's Prayer unto God" (More),
    ix, 74–76
Picus, 4
piety, xii
Pius II, Pope, 6
Plato, 8
pleasure, 61–62
poetry, vii, ix
Poliziano, Angelo, 18, 18n14
prayer, vii, xii, xv, xvi, 15, 32–33,
    41–42, 47
"Prayer to God" (Pico), ix, 74–76
pride, xvi, xvii–xviii, xviii, xx,
    8–10, 16, 31, 46, 47, 55, 57
Psalm 16, x–xi, xviii, 45–53
Psalmist, x
purgatory, xv
Pythagorus, 8

rebukes, 38–42
religious life, viii
Renaissance, viii
rhyme royal poetry, vii, ix
righteousness, 47, 48

saints, vii, 39, 45, 49, 56, 61, 65
Satan, 56, 76
Savonarola, xiv, xv, xix
Scripture, 12, 52
self-knowledge, x, xvii
Seneca, xviii, 16
service, xi, xvii, xx, 17, 18, 21,
    23, 50, 72, 73
sin, 30, 52
    spiritual battle and, 54–60
Son of God. *See* Christ

spiritual battle
    pride and, xviii
    rules of, vii, ix–x, 54–60
    weapons of, vii, x, 61–65
suffering, ix, 16, 20, 22, 24,
    38-39, 41, 55, 69

temptation, vii, ix, 30, 61–65
theology, 8
Thomas Aquinas, St., 12
Trismegistus, 8
trust, 42, 45, 47, 56, 62
truth, 39
"Twelve Properties of a Lover"
    (More), ix, xvi, 66–73
"Twelve Rules of Spiritual Battle"
    (More), ix–x, 54–60
"Twelve Weapons of Spiritual
    Battle" (More), ix, 61–65

vice, 4, 5, 12, 20, 41, 47, 50, 58
Virgil, 26–27
virtue, xiii–xiv, xv, 3–5, 11–12,
    15, 30, 39, 46, 47, 50
    of Christ, 56
    friendship and, xvi
    philosophy and, xxi, 34
    pleasure in, 31
    spiritual battle and, 54–60
    training in, vii
vocation, vii, viii, xix, 24

wisdom, 36, 40
worldly glory, 17–18